FROM MY HEART TO YOURS

Inspirational Messages from the Wives of Ministers

Compiled by Patti M. Hummel

From My Heart to Yours

Editing by
Vicki Huffman, VP/Senior Editor
The Benchmark Group LLC
benchmarkgroup2@aol. com

Published by:
The Benchmark Group LLC
148 Del Crest Drive Suite One
Nashville, TN 37217-4640
BenchmarkGroup1@aol.com

in association with:

McDougal Publishing
P.O. Box 3595
Hagerstown, MD 21742-3595
www.mcdougalpublishing.com

ISBN 978-1-58158-005-1

Printed in the United States of America
For Worldwide Distribution

FROM MY HEART TO YOURS

Inspirational Messages from the Wives of Ministers

I have listened over the years to the hearts of the wives of ministers. Their commitment to service and their concerns are powerful reminders to each of us that a call on a husband's life is also a call on his wife's life. It has been my desire to see an inspirational book made available for the host of women who could draw life lessons from ministerial wives. *From My Heart to Yours: Inspirational Messages from the Wives of Ministers* is such a book. It is full of messages from women who have often grown in the background and learned in silence. Here they share lessons that offer empathy and encouragement to those who have similar callings and a glimpse into their world to those who don't.

It is my hope that you will be refreshed in your walk with Christ Jesus as you get to know these lovely women of God. Through their transparency, you will be brought to tears, will laugh out loud, and will see your faith challenged with every turn of the page. This is a book to share, one that will be more effective every time another woman shares tender moments with a minister's wife, the often unrecognized Proverbs 31 woman.

In Christ,
Patti

My Times Are in Thy Hands

(Psalm 31:15)

Anna L. Waring (1823-1910)

Father, I know that all my life Is portioned out for me,
And the changes that are sure to come, I do not fear to see;
But I ask Thee for a present mind Intent on pleasing Thee.

I ask Thee for a thoughtful love, Through constant watching wise,
To meet the glad with joyful smiles, And to wipe the weeping eyes;
And a heart at leisure from itself, To soothe and sympathize.

I would not have the restless will That hurries to and fro,
Seeking for some great thing to do, Or secret thing to know;
I would be treated as a child, And guided where I go.

Wherever in the world I am, In whatsoe'er estate,
I have a fellowship with hearts To keep and cultivate;
And a work of lowly love to do For the Lord on whom I wait.

So I ask Thee for the daily strength, To none that ask denied,
And a mind to blend with outward life While keeping at Thy side;
Content to fill a little space, If Thou be glorified.

And if some things I do not ask, In my cup of blessing be,
I would have my spirit filled the more With grateful love to Thee—
More careful—not to serve Thee much, But to please Thee perfectly.

There are briers besetting every path, That call for patient care;
There is a cross in every lot, And an earnest need for prayer;
But a lowly heart that leans on Thee Is happy anywhere.

In a service which Thy will appoints, There are no bonds for me;
For my inmost heart is taught "the truth" That makes Thy children "free"
And a life of self–renouncing love, Is a life of liberty.

Agony of the Leaf

All discipline for the moment seems not to be joyful, but sorrowful; yet to those who have been trained by it, afterwards it yields the peaceful fruit of righteousness. Hebrews 12:11 NASB

Tea ranks second to water in America as the beverage of Choice. People are not only learning about the various types and flavors but about the health benefits of this special leaf. Having owned a tea room for five years, I have learned many interesting facts about this "liquid gold."

In learning the art of making tea, I discovered each tea requires a specific temperature of water and length of steeping to bring out the best taste. The term used for the tea in hot water is "agony of the leaf." Today's verse came to mind when I learned this term. It is not until the leaf goes through the agony of hot water that its flavor and health benefits are released. Isn't that how it is with us? We too do not yield the peaceful fruit of righteousness without going through hot water. The fragrance of the tea reaches the nose before the flavor touches the tongue. Our lives give off an aroma of righteousness when we are trained by our discipline. We are flavorful to the world around us as we come through trials.

May I suggest you prepare yourself a cup of loose leaf tea (whole leaf, if possible) and watch the leaves unfurl and release their treasures. As you sip your "cuppa," praise God for His discipline that will end in righteousness.

Mrs. Dea Irby

Father, help me to be thankful for trials and to be trained by them that I may yield the peaceful fruit of righteousness. Amen

God is Sovereign

The Lord has established His throne in the heavens; and His sovereignty rules over all. Psalm 103:19 NASB

One of the stories in the Bible that always puts a smile on my face is the story of Elisha and the Shunammite woman (2 Kings 4 and 8). He had brought her son back to life. When a famine was predicted, he told her to go abroad with her family until it was over. Seven years later she returned and went to the palace to appeal to the king to have her property reinstated. Elisha's servant Gehazi just happens to be there. On that particular day, the king wanted to hear about all of the great things Elisha had done. Gehazi was telling him about how Elisha had brought this young boy back to life and, what do you know, here they are now!The Shunammite woman had her audience with the king who gave back her land.

One of the lessons God has been teaching me freshly this year is the truth that HE IS SOVEREIGN. Three years ago we moved to Ukraine to be missionaries. We left Atlanta, GA during a driving thunderstorm. As we sat on the tarmac for two hours waiting to take off, we were very emotional about leaving our family and filled with anxiety about missing our connection and losing our luggage. Well, we *did* miss our connection and they *did* lose some of our luggage. But when we boarded the final leg of our trip, my husband was seated next to a young university student. They talked the whole way, and Zoya prayed to receive Christ before we got to Kiev!

MRS. DANELLE NELSON

Thank you that you are Lord of all and have plans formed in perfect faithfulness for us! Amen

In the World, Not of It

Do not conform any longer to the pattern of this world, but be transformed by the renewing of your mind. Romans 12:2 NIV

Shortly after beginning to serve a new church, we were invited to the wedding of a member's son. Once the wedding was over, we had two hours to wait before the reception started. Many people from our new church were at the wedding, and several invited us to a restaurant for appetizers before the reception. Desiring to get to know people, we decided to join them. I was not prepared for what I was about to experience. One couple ordered alcoholic drinks with the appetizers and much of the conversation centered on a country music concert that many present were going to attend.

All of this shocked me. Friends in our previous church had shared our convictions about entertainment. And alcohol would have never been ordered in the middle of the afternoon with us there. In the midst of our conversation, I became discouraged and questioned God. *Why had He brought us to this church?* I also thought that my convictions were going to have to change because they seemed foreign and irrelevant now. As I looked around the table, I suddenly realized it wasn't my convictions that had to change but my love for these people, so that I desired to see them fall more in love with Jesus. The Lord was reminding me that as Christ's servants we are not meant to become a part of the world but to bring the world to Him.

Mrs. Krissy Guhl

Lord, help us to be faithful witnesses of your love and grace to the fallen world. Amen

Helpmate

The LORD God said, "It is not good for the man to be alone. I will make a helper suitable for him." Genesis 2:18 NIV

After many successful years in the business world, my husband accepted a call to full-time ministry. As he returned to school to earn a degree in theology, I began to realize what his new goal was going to mean to me. The thought of becoming a pastor's wife was intriguing, although somewhat intimidating. Could I fit the bill? And what about my own career, would it still be in the picture?

It wasn't long before God convinced me that He had bigger things in store for me, too. Three people who did not know each other confirmed my new role by each using the term "helpmate" as they prayed with me for God's guidance for the future. That was enough to convince me to resign my position and concentrate on being a helpmate. The only question that remained in my mind was the job description. How exactly was I to spend my days? Together my husband and I researched the word and discovered what God wanted me to do. *Helpmate* literally means someone who is opposite and thus complements or completes another. We looked at each other and smiled, knowing that we have always kidded each other about how different we are. Here was an opportunity to use our differences for God's glory! As I have worked beside my husband in ministry over the past dozen years, I have experienced God using me to "fill the gaps" in many ways. Our ministry flows like an unbroken stream as together we accomplish the work to which we are called.

MRS. HELEN KRUDOP

Thank you for intertwining our lives with others so that You are glorified. Amen

Can God Use Me?

But the wisdom that is from above is first pure, then peaceable, gentle, and easy to be intreated, full of mercy and good fruits, without partiality, and without hypocrisy. James 3:17 KJV

When I was a child, I was so shy that I couldn't even go to Sunday school or church. If I was around people, I would throw up or pass out—sometimes both. I wanted to go to church, so I prayed for boldness and wisdom. The Lord began making changes in me. I was able to start going to church with my parents. I talked to God a lot and read my Bible. When I was older, I prayed for a godly husband who would take me to church. God answered my prayers and has grown me so much that people who know me now can't believe that I was so shy. I started serving the Lord in the nursery. Jesus has slowly moved me out of my comfort zone each step of the way, until now I have taught infants through teens. I have even been able to take a stand on something I am passionate about at church business meetings.

If we allow Him, God will use any of us, in spite of ourselves, and He will continue to grow us until the day He calls us home.

Mrs. Bonnie M. Lambert

Please fill me with wisdom and boldness to do your will and your work, in Jesus' name. Amen

Bitter or Better

Forgive as the Lord forgave you. Colossians 3:13 NIV

Years ago, a man slapped my little boy in the face for what he deemed, "a good reason." My husband and I—no matter how severe the misbehavior—had never used our hands as a means of discipline. So, needless to say, this "Mama Tiger" was HOT!

It seemed to me that it was one thing to forgive someone who was sorry. But it was quite another thing to forgive someone who felt completely justified in doing what he had done. I found myself becoming bitter, and it spilled over into many areas of my life. All the time, God wanted me to become *better* as I dealt with this circumstance He had allowed. I found that during this time, forgiveness became a process:At first, I didn't want to forgive. Then I wanted to forgive so God would "zap" him and everyone he loved. Soon I was miserable. Next I wanted to forgive because I wanted some relief from the emotional strain. Finally, I wanted to forgive because my loving Heavenly Father, who ALWAYS has my best interest at heart and desires my life to glorify Him, said to forgive. What freedom!

Mrs. Vonna S. Downs

Father, the choices are to become bitter or to become better, so please help me to choose your way of forgiveness. Amen

Feminine Warfare

...seeketh not her own, is not easily provoked, thinketh no evil
I Corinthians 13:5 KJV

The thought life is the battleground of feminine Christian warfare. It is our private conversations with ourselves that will either produce godly words and actions or will lead us into sin. How we must guard against sin in our thoughts if we would bring honor to our Savior in our lives! A prideful criticism, a stiff-necked rebellion, or feelings of fear, hurt, or jealousy; these thoughts can be as involuntary as a sneeze. But at their occurrence we will always respond. We will either reject the thought as an enemy or invite it in to be entertained as an unexpected and yet politely welcomed guest.

If we would faithfully wage war against wrong thinking we must first ACKNOWLEGE OUR SIN. So often we want to excuse sinful thoughts with "everyone has a right to have an opinion" or "it's just the truth!"But we're commanded to love as we've been loved and forgive as we've been forgiven. Secondly, we must ADORE OUR SAVIOR. Rejecting sinful thoughts is not enough. We must replace self-centered thinking with Christ-centered thinking and view people and circumstances through the lens of love for Christ. Thirdly, we must ADORN OUR SERVICE. Just as a feminine presence in a home sets the atmosphere, we as women create the aroma of the church. If we are women who are gracious and loving in our thoughts, forgiving and forbearing, humble and of a meek and quiet spirit, waiting on the Lord in trust and believing in His goodness, then our words and actions will adorn the Gospel and be a sweet smelling savor.

Mrs. Jan Kimbro

May we know the mind of Christ and may the beauty of the Lord be upon us! Amen

Just Pointing it Out

> *The one who speaks against a brot*
> *evil against the law and judges t*
> *you are not a doer of the law bu*
> *giver and judge, [He] who is able to save*
> *are you to judge your neighbor?* Jam

Not too long ago, our family went to visit a widow in our church. We had a great visit but before we left, my husband Chad wanted to pray for the dear saint. As we gathered in a circle holding hands, our nine-month-old Elijah began to babble during the prayer. Abe, our two and one-half-year old, caught on to the noise and began to shush him. Although he's usually the one making the racket, Abe thought it necessary to remind Elijah that we are to be quiet when Dad prays.

Isn't human nature funny? We want to point out the sins in others, even though they're the same sins we struggle with. Judas did this to the woman who anointed Jesus' feet. He judged her for not selling the ointment and giving the money to the poor instead of "wasting" it on the Lord's feet. And Judas was a thief! How many of us walk through the church halls judging our brothers or sisters and then later realize that we are guilty of the same offense? I chuckled at my son's hypocrisy that day. But I assure you that God does not laugh at us when we judge others for our own shortcomings.

Mrs. Melody A. Hertler

> *Perfect Judge, forgive me for pointing out the sins in others when I have no right. Amen*

...ng in the Need of Prayer

...aying always with all prayer and supplication in the Spirit, be-...ing watchful to this end with all perseverance and supplication for all the saints— and for me, that utterance may be given to me, that I may open my mouth boldly to make known the mystery of the gospel. Ephesians 6:18-19 NKJ

My husband and I were praying for wisdom to know the right approach to take with one of our teenagers. We were heavy-hearted about the child, and I mentioned our concern as a prayer request in a ladies Bible study group. After a few moments of silence, one lady said, "But the child is a preacher's kid?" I answered, "Our children are born sinners the same as yours, and they need God to work in their lives also. My husband and I need God's wisdom just as much as any parent does. Just because we are in the ministry, that doesn't make us perfect parents. We need prayer just like all parents do."

Many in our congregations think that pastors and their families are above the need for prayer. But we know differently. We know that we need God's wisdom and grace to live by His will just as everyone else does. The Apostle Paul appealed to the Ephesian church to pray for "all the saints—and for me." Paul knew that without the grace of God working in him, he would not be bold enough to preach the Gospel. If Paul needed prayer to do the will of God, how much more do all of us need it?

MRS. BETTY MICK

Lord, gives us the wisdom and grace to respond righteously to all of our family troubles. Amen

Ordinary Objects

"...when your children ask you, 'What do these stones mean?' tell them that the flow of the Jordan was cut off before the ark of the covenant of the LORD. When it crossed the Jordan, the waters of the Jordan were cut off. These stones are to be a memorial to the people of Israel forever." Joshua 4:6-8 NIV

During a vacation, one of my daughters started to gather rocks from the dirty lake where she was wading. I didn't want a bunch of dirty rocks, so I didn't allow her to bring them all home. After some drama, I allowed her to choose one. I asked her why she wanted to bring dirty rocks home, and she said it was to commemorate her vacation since she enjoyed her time at the lake so much.

When we got home, I thought about this incident. I learned something from my daughter—that it was important to remember something significant in your life. Instead of having issues with it, I should have encouraged it. Through Joshua, the Lord instructed the Israelites to do exactly that, to pick up stones and to use them as memorials, as reminders to their children of God's deliverance. Maybe we can all learn a lesson from my daughter. We should be thinking of ways to teach our children about God's work in our lives. All we have to do is look around us and use ordinary objects to teach extraordinary lessons. Even a dirty rock might do.

Mrs. Daisy Wong

Lord, please give me wisdom and insight on how to teach my children about You in a simple, ordinary way. Amen

Submitting to Suffering

The Angel of the LORD said to her, "Return to your mistress, and submit yourself under her hand." Genesis 16:9 NKJ

We view Hagar as the antagonist in the Abram-Sarai story, but she is a sufferer. Some of it she brought on herself, and some was beyond her control. Whether she wanted it or not, Hagar became a wife to Abram and conceived his child (Genesis 16:3-4). This resulted in her despising Sarai and no doubt becoming insolent." I don't have to do what you say—I'm pregnant!"When Sarai "dealt harshly" with her, she ran to the wilderness. Here the Angel of the Lord showed up for the first time in Genesis. He called her by name, recognizing her personhood and identity. What was his solution for Hagar? She must live with the conflict and submit to the suffering. But God also gave her promises: her son will beget a multitude and will hold his own against antagonists. In other words, her son will never be a slave like she is. She responds by giving God a new name: "God who sees." Her son's name will be Ishmael: "God who hears." God does not eliminate her suffering. Instead, He gives something to help her endure it: He gives Himself.

When I suffer, I also want to run away. I plead with God for its removal and demand to know why. But God gives promises not explanations. He wants me to ask "WHO are You, Lord?" not "WHY am I suffering?" Hagar teaches me to submit to what God wants, even if it means living with situations I do not like. I can do this because God sees my pain and hears my prayers.

Mrs. Marcia Hornok

Thank you for being the God who sees and hears me and who speaks to me through your Word. Amen

Preacher's Itch

...necessity is laid upon me; yes, woe is me if I do not preach the gospel! I Corinthians 9:16b NKJ

My husband preferenced his marriage proposal with, "God has called me to preach and I don't know where He will send me, but if it's the Lord's will, will you marry me?" I would and I did. We served together as student summer missionaries hundreds of miles north of our Texas home. My husband's strong desire to preach, the *preacher's itch*, led him to preach in jails and supply church pulpits. Once he hitchhiked 300 miles to be a camp pastor. While attending Bible school in Tennessee, we served as summer house parents at Bethel Bible Village Christian Children's Home to support our growing family. Upon graduation, and four children later, we resigned Bethel and moved back to Texas to pastor a mission church. It wasn't long before we were back at Bethel where Bob served as Assistant Director, and we welcomed our fifth and last child. But soon, the preacher's itch became strong again and Bob accepted the call to a Tennessee church where we witnessed the Lord use our training to minister to the congregation.

It appeared that a pattern for our lives was developing: to pastor for a season, then to return to Bethel. Two more pastorates and two more moves back to Bethel where Bob retired after twelve years as Executive Director. Now, as a north Georgia seminary Dean of Extension Schools, Bob encourages students who are experiencing the preacher's itch. He is the best person I know to guide these young men of God. Nineteen years as my favorite pastor—itch and all!

MRS. JEWEL A. MCFARLAND

Thank you, Father, for giving me the grace to follow You and my husband, as he allowed You to lead him. Amen

The Shepherd Becomes a Lamb

My God, my God, why hast thou forsaken me? Psalm 22:1 KJV

Psalm 22 is a mournful song written by King David during a period of intense distress in his life. Though scorned by man, he was confident God would not abandon him and was encouraged to keep on praying. David describes a feeling of worthlessness and defenselessness—like a worm. Many mocked and insulted him on account of his faith. Weak and seemingly on the brink of death, he compared his enemies to various types of wild animals. David's experiences have even greater significance because they describe events that are prophetic in nature and point to a death he would not suffer but his descendant, the Messiah, would. This psalm depicts a horrible execution known as crucifixion which would not be invented until centuries later by the Romans.

Can you personally relate to any of the feelings described in this psalm? Or do you relate to how David is encouraged by what God has done in the past? What is the prayer realized or the hope expressed, and how does it compare with your own vision for the future? What clues do we get from this psalm about what to do when we feel forsaken by God? Note that God rescued David from death, but God did not spare His own Son. God understands our sufferings and has the power to deliver us from them or carry us through them. Like David, this is our assurance.

Mrs. Lori Ciccanti

Thank you for the blessed hope You have given us in your Son. We shall behold His face and be satisfied when we awake with His likeness. Amen

No One to Tell

For I have no one like-minded, who will sincerely care for your state. Philippians 2:20 NKJ

What can a minister's wife do when she suspects her husband has stopped being godly? A series of setbacks had left my husband disillusioned with God (which happens to many periodically on the journey of faith). But after I prayed about this for more than a year, things seemed to be getting worse, not better. Every time I talked to my husband about his attitude, I sounded critical and self-righteous. I couldn't tell anyone in the church, lest they lose respect for their pastor. Who could I go to? Then I learned about a ministry wives' retreat that included 30 minutes with a professional counselor, if you desired it. I told my husband I wanted to go. We took money out of savings to buy airfare, and I registered for the conference. Looking back, I'm glad I went. The counselor did nothing more than remind me of Philippians 4:6-9 and pray with me, but it was worth it. I got to cry for thirty minutes and share my family secrets with a safe person.

I can't really say when my husband started getting better or even what catalyst made the difference for him, but gradually I realized he was devoted to God and the ministry once again. Sometimes praying to God about our problems does not seem like enough. We may also need to talk to ears we can see, hear counsel from a human mouth. If this means spending money to have time with a Christian counselor, in my opinion, it is worth it.

MRS. MARCIA HORNOK

Lord, when I need a like-minded person to talk to, please show me where to go. Amen

The Blessing of Barrenness

Children are a gift of the LORD... Psalm 127:3a NASB

My husband and I both wanted a Christian family with lots of children. It was devastating to learn that would not be possible because of infertility problems. We continued to pray and trust God that if He gives a desire, it is His will to satisfy those desires. We adopted our first child, a beautiful, blonde baby boy who became the heart of our home and fulfilled our prayers for a child. We prayerfully pursued what we believed was God's will for us to have another child. A beautiful dark-haired, dark-eyed baby girl has graced our lives ever since. Not wanting to be selfish but feeling once again the pull of God toward another child, we prayed and God brought a girl, dark-haired and blue-eyed, to us. We praised Him for our precious children and the blessings of learning to trust Him for our deepest desires, but God had not finished.

Some years later a physician friend called: "A baby, with some physical difficulties, was born. Do you know anyone who might adopt a handicapped child?"Our hearts were strangely drawn to adopt our fourth precious child, our second blonde, blue-eyed baby boy. His physical and mental disabilities were profound. We learned much about God's love as our immediate family, and our church family, shared that love with Benjamin for the seven and one-half years that we were blessed to have him here on earth. Philip, Hallie, Tricia, and Benjamin are cherished blessings from a God who continues to teach us to trust His provision and blessings—even when they are different from what we might have planned.

Mrs. Carol Henschel

Lord, thank you that your plan includes blessing as we learn to trust. Amen

Lonely Places

I will lead the blind by ways they have not known, along unfamiliar paths I will guide them; I will turn the darkness into light before them and make the rough places smooth. Isaiah 42:16 NIV

I have walked through lonely places, not often physically alone, yet my heart was lonely. Lord, You said in Your Word to Joshua, "I will never leave you nor forsake you." (Deuteronomy 31:6) Doesn't that promise stand for God's people today and hold true for me? I have struggled, at times, to walk through the lonely places. Slowly, the Lord has revealed sources of the loneliness that tries to settle down inside of me. Transition and change often seem to set the stage for it.

God was at work in our lives. Several years ago, I realized when my husband responded to the Lord's call into ministry that this change for him would also bring changes for me. But I never realized there would be days of extreme loneliness in my future. As churches change, so do its members. We watched as some of our closest and dearest friends left our church for one reason or another. We blessed them as they went, though selfishly we wanted them to stay with us. Something deep inside seemed to taunt, "You can't leave!You're here no matter what!You're alone now!" These are trying times for my husband and for me, yet we continue to sense that the Lord is up to something new. The way seems dark at times. I can't always sense the Lord's guidance, but He promises to make the way smooth and to bring His light into the darkest situations.

Mrs. Diane Bakk

Lord, I claim your promises: "I will lead the blind, I will guide them; I will turn the darkness into light, and make the rough places smooth." Amen

Suffering Together

And if one member suffers, all the members suffer with it; if one member is honored, all the members rejoice with it.

I Corinthians 12:26 NASB

Christians will encounter trials in this life! Those of us in ministry often get an extra dose of them. My husband and I have certainly experienced our fair share: an earthquake throwing us out of bed in the middle of the night; not having jobs, money, or a place to live; the loss of several family members; and many other difficult circumstances. As I am writing this, it is only a few days before our twins' birthday. They would be seven years old this year, however they were born prematurely and the Lord saw fit to take them to be with Him. Trials are hard!They can be particularly difficult when you are in ministry. I think we often feel like we have to be so strong and stoic, that we aren't supposed to struggle like everyone else. Surely we have the "count it all joy" thing figured out, right? Let me encourage you not to put that burden on yourself. Do not try to suffer in silence. I've been guilty many times because I didn't want others to know that I was struggling. But, I realized, that is pride.

When trials come, the first thing we should do is immerse ourselves in God's Word and prayer. The body of Christ, the church, is such a wonderful gift from the Lord. It is usually longing for a chance to encourage and support the pastor and his family. As I think back over all the trials we have been through, I can see the faces of those who surrounded us with love and support. I praise God for how He knit us together with the body of Christ during those times. If you are in the ministry, thank God for the believers the Lord has entrusted your husband and you to serve and allow them to have the blessing of serving you in return.

Mrs. Robin Yawn

Dear Lord, I thank you for the body of Christ and the privilege to serve them and be served by them. May we "count it all joy." Amen

Encouragement

For everything that was written in the past was written to teach us, so that through endurance and the encouragement of the Scriptures we might have hope. Romans 15:4 NIV

To encourage: to inspire with courage, spirit, or confidence; to stimulate by assistance, approval; to promote, advance, or foster. Wow! God's Word really does all this! Think about all the times God has given you the courage to say something or the confidence to do something. If we have God's Word hidden in our hearts, we can draw encouragement from the scriptures 24/7! The scriptures provide encouragement which gives us hope.

Being a missionary in Ukraine can be discouraging at times. I can lose courage very easily if I don't keep my eyes on Jesus and His Word in my heart. The Ukrainian people need a lot of encouragement and hope. That's why we need to be in God's Word, not only for ourselves but for others as well. We came to Ukraine to tell them about the God of hope, even though they were told He didn't exist. God uses the members of His body to minister to the rest of the body. Crossing the ocean to share the Gospel message has been worth every sacrifice to bring hope to these people. It feels good when someone encourages us; it can make our day. When we offer encouragement to another, we offer that same sense of hope to them. With all the discouraging things in the world we, Christians, can bring glory to God by being an encouragement to others. Let the encouragement of the scriptures permeate your life and be known as an encourager.

Mrs. Kenyon Powers

Lord, fill me up with your Word so others may be encouraged by the hope within me. Amen

In Quietness

In quietness and confidence shall be your strength.
Isaiah 30:15b NKJ

On countless mornings and sometimes during the day, I've glanced at a little plaque in my bathroom that contains today's Scripture. When I do, I gain strength for whatever is going on at the time. Often my prayer at those moments has been only one word: "Lord." He and I both know what I mean: *Help me, Lord, to be quiet in my spirit and renew the confidence I have in You that this task is not too big for us together!*

As a busy mother, pastor's wife, adolescent counselor and high school teacher, my days and nights have so often been a cacophony of noise, telephones ringing, and children dashing through the house, sometimes followed by the dog who is not allowed in the house. Add to that a husband's office in the house and the beeps of "call waiting"—people needing to talk, needing more than I have to give. *(Lord, once again, my simple prayer.)* It's said that Susannah Wesley, John and Charles' mother and the mother of 17 more, would cover her face with her apron to be alone with the Lord and have a few moments of quietness. She knew where her strength came from. We, busy women, caught in a whirlwind of activity and demands, must not forget the importance of finding quietness and time alone with God. Otherwise anxiety and tension will fill our homes, driving out the tender atmosphere where God's love should reign. Maybe it's time to quiet the noise in our lives. Turn off the TV and let the answering machine get the telephone. Slip away for a few minutes and be quiet, resting your burdens on Him, until renewed and strengthened with confidence, you can return.

Mrs. Jacquelyn Sheppard

Lord, I can't do this by myself. Help me find that place of quietness with You, where I can find myself in You. Amen

My Words

May the words of my mouth and the meditation of my heart be pleasing in your sight, O LORD... Psalm 19:14 NIV

I remember the first pastorate my husband and I accepted. We had three children under six years old, and I was very naïve in wanting to be the "best pastor's wife" on planet earth. It wasn't long before I began to experience how painful it can be to have your words twisted and used against you. I found out how hard it was to communicate clearly what I was trying to say without a multitude of misunderstandings. It was a rude awakening to learn that, to avoid problems, my words should be few and my listening should be much. Soon I was in despair, wanting to escape the life of a pastor's wife.

I talked with God about how I was going to survive as a pastor's wife. The Lord spoke to my heart that I could allow this season of life to destroy me or I could allow it to strengthen me. The Lord spoke to my heart, reminding me to love Him with all my heart, soul, mind, and strength and also to love my neighbor as myself. That was my assignment from my Heavenly Father and I set out with God's strength to do it. I began to seek to know Christ in a deeper way and to give unconditional love to every person I met. My heart was changing because I chose to do things God's way and not my own. Because of God's marvelous grace, my season as a pastor's wife became a time of growth and joy instead of a time of despair and defeat.

MRS. JANICE UPTON

Help me, Jesus, to use my words to encourage others as we walk together. Amen

When Silence Isn't Golden

Make a joyful noise unto the Lord, all ye lands. Psalm 100:1 KJV

December 7, 2004. The day that will live in infamy… at least in my life, it will. A two-hour operation brought me back from 18 years of progressive hearing loss to the wonderful world of hearing again. But it also was the day the music died. Cochlear implants are a medical miracle. One shortcoming, though, is their inability to restore the richness of music. Intense therapy can help but, for now, music brings back memories of an old transistor radio. Why a devotion about music dying? I was the church keyboardist for several years, and regularly went to sleep and awoke with worship music playing in my mind. Now the music was gone.

I also realized over time that my joy in Jesus was diminishing. I longed to play my piano, but the resulting noise was agonizing. So I stopped. I stopped taking in praise music. And I stopped singing. Last Christmas Eve, the tears streamed down my face as Silent Night's melody escaped me. *Lord, where are you in all of this?* This difficult, yet necessary journey has caused me to deeply search my soul. Just how dependent was I on "The BEST 100 Christian Worship Songs" to enter God's presence? Had I become so reliant on man's interpretation of praise that I couldn't worship Jesus without it? What were my motives in worship? The word "worship" was originally written "worthship." These days I pursue my quest of worship, knowing Jesus is so WORTH it. And what joyful noise awaits me when I meet Him face to face!

Mrs. Margie Campbell

"I will bless You, Lord, at all times; Your praise shall continually be in my mouth." Amen

Ministering from Home

...But as for me and my household, we will serve the LORD.
Joshua 24:15 NIV

I sensed a call from the Lord to be a compassionate nurse. As a pastor's wife in Hawaii, I found my most fulfilling ministry as a hospice nurse to the dying. It was exciting to see God open the door for witness and salvation in the homes of various cultural backgrounds. However, my husband's retirement and our move to Colorado brought this delightful ministry to an end.

It was an abrupt change from ministering to people at death's door to seeking a ministry we could have from home. God laid on our hearts the need for a big home, and we prayed, "Lord, use our home to serve You." Our heartfelt desire soon became a reality. My widowed mother came to live with us, and my hospice training is now in use. In her last days, she is surrounded by loved ones. Our teenage granddaughter, struggling with eating disorders and many issues from a broken home, came to live with us from California, and we became surrogate parents. Today, she is married to a fine Christian man and they are establishing a Christian home. Christmas finds us hosting the family get-together, and we have also served as a haven of rest for our extended family as they travel across the states. Sometimes we served as a homeless shelter, so to speak, as our children were looking for new jobs. As I look back on that innocent retirement prayer, I couldn't have realized how much God would use our home as a haven of rest. Be careful what you pray: the Lord is listening and He delights to answer.

Mrs. Charlotte Boaz

Lord, help us remember that perhaps our greatest ministry is from our beloved home. Amen

The Important Thing

"Martha, Martha...one thing is needed." Luke 10:41-42 NKJ

A magazine photographer wanted to get photos of a huge forest fire. He called his home office to hire a plane. "It will be waiting for you at the airport," his editor assured him. When he arrived at the small airport, a plane was warming up. He jumped in with his equipment and yelled, "Let's go!" The pilot swung the plane into the wind and took off. "Fly over the north side of the fire," said the photographer, "and make three or four low-level passes." "Why?" asked the pilot. "Because I'm going to take pictures!" yelled the photographer, wondering why he had to explain. After a long pause the pilot said, "You mean you're not the flight instructor?"

Like the harried photographer, many times I become so focused on a frantic pursuit, that I neglect the most important thing. In my case, that's my relation to God and to people. Some days I hit the bedroom floor running and collapse back into bed at night, only to realize I have scarcely thought about God all day. Other times I get so adrenaline-driven working on a project that I neglect the needs of my husband and children. No matter how urgent or compelling my circumstances, if I take off without God at the controls, it will be like flying in the wrong direction with a pilot who does not know how to land. God created me for fellowship with Him. Trying to serve Him in the flesh blocks that fellowship. Even though Martha's work was necessary, Jesus affirmed Mary for sitting at His feet and listening to His words.

Mrs. Marcia Hornok

Please enable me to do Martha's duties with Mary's devotion. Amen

Respectable Sins

She openeth her mouth with wisdom; and in her tongue is the law of kindness. Proverbs 31:26 KJV

As my husband and I were traveling, we heard a radio program discussing how Christians believe that all sins are considered equal in God's eyes but often more deceptive sins—one of which is gossip—the church finds acceptable. This ignited a discussion between us. Today with thousands of gossip magazines and tabloids, gossip has become a gigantic profit-making industry. We also see the sin of gossip frequently in cyberspace. We have been inundated with all kinds of forwards and e-mails that, simply stated, are full of malicious gossip.

The book of Titus warns older women not to be malicious gossips or slanderers but to be reverent in the way they live. Webster defines "malicious" as a desire to harm others or to see others suffer. Why do Christians feel they have the right to say things about people they don't know and pass on information that they do not know is valid with the intent to harm them? The answer lies in the fact that we do not see the sin of gossip through God's eyes. When we do, we will take to heart Paul's words in Ephesians 4:29-30 NIV: "Do not let any unwholesome talk come out of your mouths, but only what is helpful for building others up according to their needs, that it may benefit those who listen…and do not grieve the Holy Spirit of God."

Mrs. Janice Upton

Dear Jesus, help me to open my mouth with wisdom and speak with kindness. Amen

It's about Time

But I trust in you, O LORD; I say "You are my God." My times are in your hands. Psalm 31:14-15a NIV

How many times I've looked at the clock and exclaimed, "It can't be that time already!Where has the time gone?" Those clock hands seem to be an enemy. However, I've been encouraged again and again by the wondrous fact that my times are in the hands of my loving God. Even before time began, God had planned my ways with my good and His glory in mind (Ephesians 1:4-6). When some of those times in my life have not seemed to make sense (polio when I was starting training to be a missionary?), God has so graciously shown His mercies. I received His peace and others were encouraged to see His faithfulness. The Holy Spirit has faithfully brought to my mind, in the times needed, the truths revealed in Ephesians chapter one and many other passages of His Word.

Time moves along even as you read these thoughts, and the hours of this coming day may seem too full and too rushed (sinks full of dishes, carpooling, committee meetings, etc.). You may have to prioritize, possibly saying "No" to some requests. But even when your time gets interrupted, keep the eyes of your heart on the One who has promised (1 Thes. 5:24) to work in and through you for His good purposes.

MRS. CAROLYN LYON

Heavenly Father, help me to fulfill faithfully your will in the time you've planned for me today. Amen

The Comparison Trap

For we dare not class ourselves or compare ourselves with those who commend themselves. But they, measuring themselves by themselves, and comparing themselves among themselves, are not wise.
2 Corinthians 10:12 NKJ

My husband and I recently attended a two-day conference for ministry workers, in particular, pastors and the wives of pastors. In addition to renewing old friendships and acquaintances, we enjoyed meeting new people and hearing about the successes and challenges of others in the ministry. At first, it was interesting to hear what our friends had been doing since we last met. I listened intently to stories of church growth or decline, doctrinal and staff issues, financial struggles, and sadly even congregational betrayal. I vacillated between relief, that our ministry problems weren't as great as some, and envy that our church was not experiencing the growth that others had.

I wondered why God wasn't using us like I thought He should. I began to question our methods, our music, and our gifts and talents. I realized that I had stepped right into the old trap of comparison. And a trap is exactly what it is. Comparisons breed pride, jealousy, envy, discouragement, and discontentment. There will always be a ministry that is growing faster, has better music, more programs, and larger salaries. I had to remind myself that it is not wise to either commend myself to or compare myself with anyone else. I must desire only commendation from the Father; I must only compare myself to what and who God wants me to become in Christ. God is using me, and He has a plan for my life that is totally unique for me.

Mrs. Mary Englund Murphy

Heavenly Father, forgive me for wanting to be anything other than what You want me to be in Christ. Amen

In His Hands

But now, O LORD, thou art our father; we are the clay, and thou our potter; and we all are the work of thy hand. Isaiah 64:8 KJV

I love to make things with clay. I took an art class as a teacher one summer. The professor said, "Create as you work." So I began working with my clay, squeezing it to get the air bubbles out. The clay became warm to my hands and more pliable. Then I was able to begin creating a form. God is that way. As we yield and become obedient to His will, we become like warm clay in His hands. Then and only then can He begin to mold us and make us into what He wants us to be.

As a teacher, I often bought clay from a nearby potter. My children loved the days we would make things from clay. The students designed their own little pots. Then they would sign the bottom with their initials. They were so proud of their work. One day a student had tears in his eyes as he showed me that he had made a mess of his pot. I showed him how to form a ball again, wet his fingers, and start all over. We are to be like clay in the Master's hands and let God be the Potter. Even when we make a mess of our creation, if we're willing to give it over to God, He is able to remake it.

Mrs. Betsy McSwain

O God, may we be willing to be molded into your design. Amen

Serving: A Way of Life

If anyone speaks, he should do it as one speaking the very words of God. If anyone serves, he should do it with the strength God provides, so that in all things God may be praised through Jesus Christ. I Peter 4:11 NIV

In the years of preparation for our church-planting ministry in Germany, there was a touch of euphoria about being missionaries. Early on the Lord brought me back to the reality that this ministry is all about serving. As a missionary wife and mother, the majority of my ministry has been serving the Lord by serving others through hospitality. This has taken me out of my comfort zone and I have learned to do this with the ability which God supplies. My practical nature leans toward getting the job done so that I must continually battle the tendency to put the job before the people. Because we serve in a culture that is not known for its loving nature, a kind word and an open home can provide a wonderful opportunity to give testimony to the love of God through Jesus Christ. The Holy Spirit has been teaching me that His divine purpose can be accomplished even in the smallest act of serving.

Ask the Lord to show you where you can minister to others. Serving to the glory of God is a way of life.

MRS. ELLEN MILLER

Heavenly Father, teach me how to serve so that in all things You will be glorified. Amen

Why me, God?

He was...a man of sorrows, and familiar with suffering.
Isaiah 53:3 NIV

"Where is God when it hurts?" "Why do bad things happen to good people?" "If God exists, why is there so much pain?" "If He loves me, why does He allow me to hurt so much?" The problem of pain is timeless and universal. People have always questioned how a loving and powerful God could allow pain and suffering. We ask the inevitable questions:What could I have done differently? Why me? And we doubt ourselves: I deserved this…if only I'd had more faith. Loved ones often add to the burden with comments intended to comfort. Job's friends insisted he must have done something wrong. Pharisees asked a man born blind how his parents sinned. Some say: "If you have enough faith, you will be healed." "All things work for good." "God didn't do this to you; He only allowed it to happen." These comments ring hollow when we suffer, and we receive no more comfort than Job's friends gave him. When we suffer, we try to make sense of it, create meaning from the experience. Our search for answers often turns to judgment. We judge those in pain, or worse, we judge God, making Him to be less than He is, minimizing His power, pretending He's not in control. The truth is that nothing happens beyond God's reach. Nothing escapes Him.

So what do we do with this problem of pain? We cling to who God is. God did not give Job a comprehensible answer to why he suffered. He simply reminded Job of who He is. We may ask questions, but we must not expect to receive (or understand) the answer.

MRS. JEANNINE LIEBMANN

Gracious God, comfort us with the reality that You are not distant and silent, but the One who became human and suffered with us. Amen

The Joy of Delegating

The body is a unit, though it is made up of many parts; and though all its parts are many, they form one body. So it is with Christ.
1 Corinthians 12:12 NIV

As pastors' wives, it is easy for us to become so involved in the church that we stop taking care of ourselves. Like many, I sought to be the perfect pastor's wife by doing all the things that weren't being done. It wasn't until I was diagnosed with thyroid cancer that I was forced to evaluate all the things I was involved in. I began to realize that I was doing too much and was not allowing others to help. As I cut back, others began to take on responsibilities. As a result, after I received a clean bill of health, I was able to focus on a few things and found that I was able to be even more effective in ministry.

In our desire to be supportive of a husband's ministry, we can be so involved that we hinder the growth of others. When we delegate responsibilities to others, we have the joy of seeing God work through them. We can watch them grow in their faith. Instead of taking on more responsibilities when people approach us with needs, we can encourage them to get personally involved. If it is an important part of the ministry, we can trust God to place upon the heart of others the need to volunteer. We need to avoid the trap of doing things just because it needs to be done. Instead, we need to focus on doing only what God has called and equipped us to do.

Mrs. Rebecca Daman

Dear Lord, help us to know our limits and allow others to experience the joy of ministry. Amen

Gates of Teeth

Out of the same mouth come praise and cursing. My brothers, this should not be. James 3:10 NIV

A tiny needle can prick a vein, causing much pain. A small bridle in a horse's mouth can steer that large animal in any direction. A small organ called the tongue can determine man's reputation and in turn destroy or build up others. When I was a child someone once told me, "If your tongue was such an innocent thing, then why did God hide it between gates of teeth?" With our tongue, we hold the power to encourage or destroy another. Being the wife of a minister, as well as in ministry myself, I have many times struggled with the aspect of holding my tongue. When my husband has been unfairly criticized or when I've seen him disappointed by the actions of others, I have been thankful for those "gates of teeth!"

The careless words of others can inflict insurmountable pain upon us. How do we respond in turn? Rather than returning criticism with criticism or pain for pain, I would encourage you to take your pain first to God. On numerous occasions, God has heard my anger, fear and frustration about others. Amazingly, I feel just as good about "getting it out," yet I do not have to deal with the consequences of unleashing my tongue where it is inappropriate. Instead of following our natural response when the unbridled tongue of another person hurts us, we need to bring it to the Lord.

Mrs. Lorie Looney Keene

Father, let our words first be sifted through You prior to being spilt out upon another. Amen

Past Her Sin

And many of the Samaritans of that city believed on him for the saying of the woman which testified, He told me all that I ever did.
John 4:39 KJV

He loved her!Jesus had looked into her dry, barren life and met her at her greatest need…she thirsted. The story of the Samaritan woman begins at a well, and ends gloriously with heaven in view. This woman, known by all of those in Samaria because of her sins, goes to Jacob's well to draw herself a drink of water. Yet, today, this Samaritan woman meets Jesus at the well. Can you imagine her embarrassment, astonishment, and shame when Jesus points out the intimate details of her life? But Jesus doesn't reject her, as she has most assuredly been rejected over and over again by friends, family, and neighbors. Jesus looks past her sin to her need.

Can you remember when you first had a personal encounter with Christ? When I was a teenager, I came to understand that Jesus loved ME. The reality of Christ's love pierced my heart with such joy that I wanted to shout! Suddenly, I couldn't read enough of His Word, my prayer life exploded with anticipation, and I wanted to share this great hope with everyone I met. But what happens to us over the years? As pastors' wives, we often are suffocated by a sea of troubles, sinful worries, and busyness. We forget the joy of our salvation. We must renew our call to share with a barren, parched world that Jesus loves them. He loves them so much that He refuses to leave them hopeless. He offers *"water springing up to eternal life"* (John 4:14).

Mrs. Debbie Brunson

Father, help us to focus on a world that is lost and barren without Jesus, the Living Water. Amen

God's Special Gift

Sons are a heritage from the LORD, children a reward from Him.
Psalm 127:3 NIV

Psalm 127 illustrates the need for complete dependence upon God in building His church, our homes and society. Without Him, our labor is in vain. Children are described as our reward and heritage for the future. This psalm may have a deeper significance to those of us who are faced with unique challenges and struggles of caring for children with disabilities. Although God does not reveal reasons for specific circumstances, we can learn from Scripture (2 Cor. 1:3-7; James 1:2-3) that our situations can be transformed by God's power and grace and in turn be a blessing to others. Some parents at a support group were once asked about the contributions their handicapped children have made in their lives. Some thoughts they shared included dependence upon God, loving unconditionally, appreciation for what comes from the heart–not just the mind, meeting people they would never have otherwise met, compassion and perseverance. It is a great privilege to have a special needs child entrusted to us by the Lord. Through faith we can be assured God has a plan and purpose for him. It is a great honor to accept this special gift and blessing from God.

- What are some concerns of special needs families and how can Psalm 127 be an encouragement?
- In what ways does God give us wisdom to help His children reach their full potential and use the gifts He has provided? How does the Lord guide and prepare us for the challenges ahead?

Building a successful home requires total dependence and trust in God.

Mrs. Lori Ciccanti

Lord, help us to surrender our lives to your will. Amen

Seeing Clearly Now

For our struggle is not against flesh and blood, but against the rulers, against the authorities, against the powers of this dark world and against the spiritual forces of evil in the heavenly realms.
Ephesians 6:12 NIV

"Why do people sometimes see only the negative things instead of the positive?" my husband asked after a long day of ministering at one of the churches we've served. Discouraged, he shared criticisms he'd encountered. One person pointedly and publicly criticized his ministry choices for that week. Another spewed rudeness, and the list went on. We loved our church, but negative attitudes had begun to spread like a nasty virus. It spread to me, too. Anger infected my heart as I listened to my husband. Usually I'm loving and merciful, slow to anger. Lash out at a loved one though, and my fruits of the spirit become rotten tomatoes I mentally hurl at the accuser. As I stewed in my resentment, God convicted me with love. He handed me a pair of spiritual eyeglasses, reminding me to gaze at others through His eyes. The flesh and blood I focus on isn't the real enemy. The real villain is the true accuser—the "powers of this dark world…the spiritual forces of evil." The Enemy delights when he deflects my anger that should be directed toward him onto a brother or sister in Christ. But when I look through God's eyes, I see truth: all Christians make mistakes (including me). They are not the enemy.

Do you struggle with hurt caused by other Christians? Ask God to give you His eyeglasses. He'll help you look at others through eyes of forgiveness. Then you'll be free to fight the real battle.

Mrs. Alison Bryant

Jesus, help me to see others through Your eyes, not as enemies, but as brothers and sisters. Amen

Peace in the Valleys

As the deer pant for streams of water, so my soul pants for you, O God. Psalm 42:1 NIV

In the beginning of my Christian life, I always heard people talk about their "mountaintop" experiences with God. Being a Montana native and a current resident of Colorado, I know a bit about mountain tops: they're cold, usually don't have a lot of trees, and the wind seems to blow all the time. The valleys however are quite the contrast: plush green meadows of grass, cool running streams of water, plenty of shade offered by countless trees, and the wind is definitely much calmer. As I became an older, wiser Christian, I began to realize that I was closer to God during the lower points of my life. I cried out to Him more often and more fervently when I was in a valley. When I was forced to be still from either physical weakness or stress built up from being a mother, working a part-time job, and being the wife of a prison chaplain, I reached some low points. But I found those were the best times because God and I had a lot of time together.

I have a framed print on my guest bedroom wall with one of my favorite sayings: "Take time for the quiet moments, as God whispers, and the world is loud." It's quiet in the valley with maybe a light breeze, the soft sound of running water. And I, like the deer, come here often to feed.

Mrs. Nona Odom

Father, thank You, for mountaintop experiences that originate in the valleys. Amen

Dressed for Battle

Finally, my brethren, be strong in the Lord and in the power of His might. Put on the whole armor of God, that you may be able to stand against the wiles of the devil. Ephesians 6:10-11 NKJ

As a young Christian, I felt intimidated and inadequate, questioning whether I would make a good Christian soldier. I knew about our godly weapons, but I didn't fully comprehend their true power. I was confident about the helmet of salvation, for I had accepted Christ as my Savior when I was twelve years old. As a teenager, I learned to share my faith clearly with others, so I knew my feet were shod with the preparation of the gospel. But what about the belt of truth, the breastplate of righteousness, the shield of faith, and the sword of the Spirit? How was I to put on the armor and use the weapons? I decided to list the armor and weapons and see what the Scriptures had to say about each one. I found:

- John 14: 6 —Jesus is the truth.
- 2 Corinthians 5:21 —our righteousness is in Christ.
- 2 Corinthians 15:1-4 —the death, burial, and resurrection of Jesus Christ is the gospel.
- Hebrews 12:2 —the author and finisher of our faith is Jesus Christ.
- Luke 2:30 —Jesus is our salvation.
- John 1:1-2 and 14 —Jesus Christ is the Word in the flesh.

Jesus doesn't just *provide* our armor, our weapons, our strength, and our power; he is our armor, our weapons, our strength and our power. When I clothe myself in Christ, I am ready for battle.

Mrs. Mary Englund Murphy

Father, thank you for providing and for being all the weapons and armor I'll ever need. Amen

Until They Ask "Why?"

Always be prepared to give an answer to everyone who asks you to give the reason for the hope that you have. But do this with gentleness and respect. I Peter 3:15b NIV

Meet Marsha, a grown-up preacher's daughter, whose parents modeled loving others in Jesus' name. Now 40-something, she lives at such risk in a third-world country that I may not even share her real name because there openly sharing about Jesus is illegal. Only if someone asks may she talk about Him. Marsha ministers in that dark world to prostitutes, women who sell their bodies in order to feed their families. During the daytime she visits these desperate women and gradually develops friendships. She asks about their families, problems, and interests. Occasionally she brings food or personal items. She expresses concern and offers help in time of sickness. Eventually one will ask, "Why do you do this?" Then she tells them of Jesus, of His love for her and for them. One by one, they are trusting Him as Savior. As they come out of that degrading lifestyle, Marsha helps them to learn job skills to earn income while she teaches them God's Word and helps them gain self-esteem.

Reaching out to unlovely persons will make us different from others. In our "me-first" world of greed and hatred and cynicism, people notice love. Look around you. Someone in your busy day-to-day world is desperate, needing Jesus' love. To whom will you put love in action until she asks "Why?"

Mrs. Janet T. Hoffman

Lord, as I encounter people without You who are desperate and dying for lack of genuine love, give me the grace to love them until they ask "Why?" and then to share Jesus. Amen

Delightful Desires

Delight yourself in the LORD; and He will give you the desires of your heart. Psalm 37:4 NASB

This verse always troubled me. I wondered if the reason the desires of my heart were not being fulfilled was that I was not really delighting in the Lord. Or were my desires not even from the Lord? Studying the passage I began to see this is one in a list of imperatives: 'Trust in the Lord, do good, dwell in the land, cultivate faithfulness, delight yourself in the Lord, commit your way to Him, trust also in Him, rest in the Lord, wait patiently for Him, fret not yourself." The "desires of your heart" speaks of the desires God gives us for people and ministry as we delight in Him. All He asks is that we commit them right back to Him. Ironically, these commands are all passive—trust, rest, and wait. Instead, we actively choose to doubt, fret, and worry.

I heard a story about a father who took his daughter to the store and bought her a balloon to carry while they were shopping. However, she accidentally let the balloon slip through her fingers. She began to cry. The father got another balloon but this time tied it to the cart. After a time he noticed that his daughter had a white-knuckled grip on the balloon string, so he showed her how the balloon was securely tied to the cart. He said, "Don't worry—Daddy has it." Our heavenly Father always has it. All we can control is our own attitude. How tightly are we going to hold onto things instead of onto Him?

Miss Leah Hornok

Father, help me delight in You and entrust the desires You give to my heart back to You. Amen

To Preach the Word

...preach the word; be ready in season and out of season; reprove, rebuke, exhort, with great patience and instruction. For the time will come when they will not endure sound doctrine; but wanting to have their ears tickled, they will accumulate for themselves teachers in accordance to their own desires... II Timothy 4:2-3 NASB

The challenge from my late husband's early years at Columbia Bible College was, "To know Him and to make Him known." And that was his hearts desire. He worked his way through college and then Dallas Theological Seminary. For much of his time in school he did not have a car, so he hitchhiked several times from Texas to Florida to visit family and friends. All the while his heart was focused on preaching the gospel message on the mission field. Being ordained, he was sometimes asked to fill in at churches and was always honored that the Lord would allow him the privilege to share the good news.

We met some years later after Don's life desire had come to a halt because he had been diagnosed with cancer. What would life have been like if he could have fulfilled that call, that desire? Cancer brings with it suffering, misery, treatments, and in Don's case, all of that completely altered his life. When we married, his life expectancy was about two years with little to no hope of having children. I loved him and was willing to be his wife no matter what. Although he did not serve a church, Don had congregants, made up of everyone who met with him. God gave us twelve years together and blessed us with three children who have been left with a powerful legacy. Despite his shortened lifespan, Don did preach the Word, putting into practice the challenge: "To know Him and to make Him known."

Ms. Patti M. Hummel

Father God, your plans are for good. Thank you for the blessing of being married to a man who had a pastor's heart. Amen

Authentic Singing

Keep your tongue from ... speaking deceit. Psalm 34:13 NASB

We really have only one major rule in our house: Do Not Lie! If you think you will get in trouble for doing something, you probably will. But if you lie to get out of it, you double your trouble! At our house, authenticity is highly regarded in words and actions. This, of course, extends outside the house. When one of our sons was about three, we were singing praise songs in church. He loved to sing (he is now in music ministry) and always joined in. We were standing singing "I Exalt Thee" and I noticed that he was sitting, arms crossed with a scowl on his face. I chastised him, "Sing, Seth!" He responded, "No!" I ordered, "Yes!" Then in his defense he said, "But I'm not exhausted!" Ohhh!

That experience came to mind the other day in church when we were singing about kneeling before the Lord. I had a mental struggle going on: *How can I sing this standing up? Should I kneel? What would people think?...It shouldn't matter what people think!...Isn't it just a matter of my heart kneeling before God anyway?...Or was that a lie of the enemy to make me compromise what God may be telling me?...I want my words to be truthful, Lord.*

My brain hurt so I decided that I should quietly, albeit on the front row, kneel down. I did. In the future, I may or may not physically kneel every time we sing about kneeling, but my heart will kneel and my lips will sing truth.

MRS. DEA IRBY

Lord, help me to be so involved in the words that I sing that I sing in truth and authenticity. Amen

Praying for You—Really!

Because He has inclined His ear to me, therefore I shall call upon Him as long as I live. Psalm 116:2 NASB

My Dad became a pastor when I was eight years old. One of the many things I learned growing up was that prayer had a priority in the Christian's life. I remember many times when there was a phone call from someone in the congregation or a need in our own family, my Dad would call us all together for a time of prayer. As a young child that spoke volumes to me. It is something that I think about often and try to model in my life with my own children.

It is easy for us to talk about prayer but not practice the discipline of it in our everyday lives. I have found myself telling people that they will be in my prayers, only to walk away from the situation and forget about it until later in the week. I was convicted of this when someone told me they would be praying for me, and I wondered if they really would. Worse is when a friend has come up to me and told me of an answer to prayer and said, "I know that you've been praying for me, and..." Now I find it very helpful to pray with someone at the time they ask for prayer (or mention that they are going through a difficult time). I also try to write it down. This helps me remember the person and the need, and later I am able to go back and ask them specifically about the situation. I think this ministers more to people than just telling them that you will be praying for them.

MRS. VICKI WOODS

Father, help me to be unselfish as I remember the needs of others and uphold them in prayer. Amen

The Gospel Message (Part I)

Jesus said, "Let the children come to Me." Matthew 19:13-15

I recall as a 3-year-old I sat on the end of a low bench with my peers in the back of our little rural church. Our teacher sat right in front of me and looked straight into my eyes and said, "God loves you." That news made me happy. I wanted tell of God's love to every child: that Jesus loved me and, what I learned later, that He said "Let the children come to Me." My excitement led me to invite children near my home to come over so I could share this news with them. Later, in my teens, I taught children in my church and was blessed to see their joy.

In response to our pastor's sermons, I soon felt called to teach children in other lands who had not been exposed to the good news of Jesus and His love for them. I enrolled in Columbia Bible College in preparation for that ministry. Almost immediately upon my arrival in Columbia, SC, I met a young man, Elmer Bonnette, who was also called to go to the mission field to spread the good news of God's love. We were married and our mission board sent us to Bangladesh to spread the gospel that God had given us. It was our desire to obey Him, but we reaped the benefits as we saw others accept Him. The Holy Spirit called us, opened our hearts to His call, and allowed us to be His servants of the gospel. Even in a foreign land, Jesus' message to children was the same, "Let them come to Me."

Mrs. Virginia Bonnette

Thank you, God, for the good news that needs to be spread more today than ever before—for the harvest is plentiful, but the laborers are few. Amen

The Gospel Message (Part II)

Go Ye... *Matthew 28:19 KJV*

While serving in Bangledash my pastor husband Elmer became very ill, and we were forced to return to the states. God was in that move and the desire He had laid on our hearts to share the gospel was given new vitality as Elmer began to gain new strength. God led us to serve churches in SC and GA. My job was as a homemaker and teacher ofchildren, still blessed to spread the gospel message. That was where I fitted. It has been such a joy to see children, our own and others, come to trust Jesus as their Savior. And how sweet through the years to see them growing in the Lord and leading others to Him in obedience to Jesus' command—"Let the children come to Me and forbid them not, for such is the Kingdom of Heaven." And as grown-ups we are still His children. And He is still calling young and old to come to Him as Savior.

The simple message of the gospel never changes, but it must be made available. What a privilege to be able to sing, "Jesus loves the little children of the world" whatever their age, size or nationality. Every Christian has the same call on their lives to GO YE and preach the good news. It could be in a foreign land or in a classroom or it could be to your own children. Go ye!

MRS. VIRGINIA BONNETTE

We have the message; help us, Lord, to spread it for your kingdom. Amen

Gifts from Above

I have no greater joy than to hear that my children are walking in the truth. *III John 4 NIV*

How in the world will I cope with three young children under three years old and be a pastor's wife, mother, and missionary? At the age of thirteen, I had given my life to the Lord to become a missionary in Africa. In my early years of marriage, I struggled with my dream to be a missionary in a far-away land. My plans were not being fulfilled. I cried out to God in my anguish "Please, God, help me not to resent the little ones you have given me; help me to love them." Now as I look back over thirty plus years, the Lord answered my prayer lavishly. Our three adult children deeply love and serve the Lord. We have six wonderfully delightful grandchildren. My children and grandchildren are treasured gifts from above.

Years ago the Lord showed me that my first mission field was my family. While serving Him in my home, the Lord gave me a heart of joy and thankfulness. I was able to watch and pray for my children to become lovers of God. There is no greater joy than to see your children walk with God. But God was not finished with my dream to be a missionary in Africa. In 2003 He said: now is the time for you to go to Africa. My husband and I were able to go on a short-term mission trip to Kenya. It took more than forty years to see the fulfillment of a young teenager's dream to go to Africa to tell others about Jesus. But God did not forget.

Mrs. Janice Upton

Dear Jesus, thank you for your faithfulness that showed me as a young mother how to love and pray for my children. Amen

Don't Worry, Be Joyful

"...the joy of the LORD is your strength" Nehemiah 8:10b NIV

While in Bible College I learned the common acronym for JOY was: Jesus —Others—Yourself. It helped me understand what was important to God. The Nehemiah passage deals with the rebuilding of the temple and the reading of the "Book of the Law of Moses which the LORD had commanded for Israel." The people were told "not to mourn or weep" but to "celebrate with great joy because they now understood the words that had been made known to them." In my zest to share Christ with others, I find individuals not receptive to the words of the Bible. I also want to share the joy of the Lord with other Christians who are having struggles with their daily Christian walk. Paul encourages us "to make my joy complete by being like-minded, having the same love, being one in spirit and purpose" (Philippians 2:2 NIV). This further explains how we can share in His joy.

Happiness is an emotion that can come or go depending on the circumstances. But an attitude of joy expresses your trust in God no matter the circumstances. Joy is like a smile in your heart while the rest of the world is falling apart. You can be joyful because Jesus is the same yesterday, today, and tomorrow. People will always let you down, but Jesus lifts you up. He will give you the ability to go through any valley, to deal with any problem. So be joyful in the Lord; it beats being happy.

MRS. SHIRLEY J. ELLIS

Lord, You are my joy, my strength in whom I can trust always. Amen

Fine Dining

Your words were found, and I ate them, and Your word was to me the joy and rejoicing of my heart; for I am called by Your name, O LORD God of host. Jeremiah 15:16 NKJ

I attended a conference for minister's wives where we were asked, "What are the best and the worst things about being a pastor's wife? "I immediately thought of a lot of the worst things. The first woman to respond to the best thing said, "My husband!"After a few moments of reflection, I realized the best thing about ministry for me is my intimacy with God. As a pastor's wife for over twenty years, I have come to know God in a way that I don't believe I would have known Him if not for the challenges of ministry. I have come to know God by devouring His word. I don't just read His word; I crave it! The Bible has become my nourishment for life.

When I need compassion, I read the gospels and try to model the compassion of Christ. When I find myself in a strange place (with strange people), I read about Ruth and her journey to an unknown land. If I don't understand why, I cry out with the psalmist. When I need encouragement, I read Zephaniah 3:17: "The LORD your God is in your midst, The Mighty One, will save; He will rejoice over you with gladness, He will quiet you with His love, He will rejoice over you with singing." I know God more intimately by dining on His word. I rejoice over the time I get to spend with God in His word.

Mrs. Karen A. Dishman

Lord, thank you for the Bible. May I never grow hungry from lack of dining on your words. Amen

Whiter than Snow

Therefore, if anyone is in Christ, he is a new creation; the old has gone, the new has come! II Corinthians 5:17 NIV

We gazed at the yard as fluffy flakes enrobed everything. Our dog preferred to run around in it instead of watching. She bounded around the white yard, slowed, and then abruptly buried her nose. This started a launch sequence. With a miniature mountain on her nose, she would take off like a NASCAR driver, racing in circles. Soon the yard looked like a snowy version of crop circles. Before she was unleashed on the untouched snow, everything looked perfect. Have you noticed how snow beautifies and highlights things normally unseen? For example, every day I used to pass an ordinary tree. I passed it hundreds of times, but I rarely noticed it. It might as well have been invisible (although I love trees). But a couple of times a year something magical happened. A dusting of snow would grace the land, and that tree became breathtaking. Each individual, delicate branch was showcased because of the dazzling white. I wondered at not noticing the tree more often, and I smiled at the sight.

Just as snow can transform a landscape, God can transform us. On our own, we are quite ordinary—like that tree. Nothing special. But as soon as we came into a relationship with God, He transformed us. Our loving Father showered on us the costly, whiter-than-snow gift of His righteous love. We became different. And like the tree, who we *really* are becomes undeniable. We are who *He* created us to be all along, created for the purpose of showcasing His glory. And He smiles at the sight.

Mrs. Alison Bryant

Father, thank you for covering us with your transforming love. Amen

Growing up Fast

...for of such is the kingdom of heaven. Matthew 19:14b KJV

What does Jesus mean when He says we should come as "little children?" That we should be "childlike"? Words like "trusting" and "loving" and "unpretentious" and maybe even "unsophisticated" come to mind. Is there anything as lovely as a little child who climbs up in your lap wanting to be cuddled, wanting nothing more than just to be close to you? Jesus may have had all this and more in mind. However, there's another attribute of childhood that I'd like to mention. Have you noticed that a little child always wants to go on to the next step of growth, unless of course, it's potty training! He watches his big brother ride a bike, and he wants to try. Never mind that he's not big enough. He wants to try, even if he falls. Eventually his own growth and maturity will be sufficient for him to ride a bike. The falls will be forgotten when he's racing down the hill. Likewise, baby sister wants to be like her mother or sister. She strives forward, seeking to act and to be "big."

I wonder if Jesus had in mind that we ought to strive to be more mature, even when we're still at the brat stage in our Christian living—that stage where we're easily offended, disappointed, angered, and discouraged. Was He encouraging us to be like a little child, wanting to grow up fast? It's not birthdays that make us more mature in Christ. It's obedience. We can still be infants and toddlers in our old age, never racing down the hill with Jesus, still in our strollers. Or we can seek to be more like our "Big Brother" our Lord, Jesus Christ.

Mrs. Jackie Shepherd

Jesus, I want to be more like You, in all my ways growing in all your ways. Amen

Ministry of Togetherness

The man and his wife were both naked, and they felt no shame.
Genesis 2:25 NIV

Oftentimes the work of ministry can be so overwhelming that pastors and their wives forget about their first ministry, home. It is not until the ugly head of intimate separation rears itself that we realize what has happened. It is very important for pastors and their wives to keep the home fires burning passionately. This is to say there should be an unbreakable, intimate connection between a husband and wife that is inclusive of spirit, mind, and body. Notice the intentional list order. A solid spiritual connection makes the atmosphere conducive for all other connections to flourish. Christ is the firmest of foundations. The question now becomes how can the ministry of togetherness be achieved and maintained? We find the answer in Genesis 2:25.

God brought this Scripture to mind as I ministered to an unmarried couple who had decided to move in together. In counseling them against that choice, God reminded me of the mistakes my husband and I had made even as a married couple. We were not "naked and unashamed." God showed me that two can never be one if there are obstacles of secrecy between them. Women across America are cringing as they read this because our mothers taught us not to share all of our "little" secrets with our husbands. However, the Bible clearly shows us that we must reveal ourselves completely to one another without shame. Trust the heart of your husband. Don't be afraid to let him in on all of you. When you are truly rooted in Christ, the result will be wholeness in your marriage.

MRS. B. MICHELLE PATILLO

God bless the ministry of togetherness. Amen

Pruned if You Do, Pruned if You Don't

...and every branch that bears fruit, He prunes it so that it may bear more fruit. John 15:2b NASB

I have a black thumb. I guess it would help if I watered the plants. But I can count on God and His green thumb. In my ladies Bible study group, "Yahweh Sisterhood," we have come up with the expression "pruned if you do, pruned if you don't" because it seems that sometimes it doesn't matter what you do, trials come. It is comforting to remember that God really is in charge and His ways are not our ways. When things make no sense to us, they do to God. When our prayers are not answered the way we think they should be, they have been answered according to Gods plan. When we feel unjustly treated or misunderstood, God knows our pain. When we feel betrayed by fellow believers, Jesus sticks closer than a brother. When it seems that the "righter" I live the "lefter" I feel, I am not alone; God is there.

God is the ultimate vine dresser who owns the vineyard and wants to protect the vine and make it produce the best fruit. The vine must yield to the Gardener who knows the right season and the amount of pruning that is necessary. The ultimate goal is to bear fruit which glorifies God, not to live a pain-free life. Keep this in mind the next time you are tempted to say, "It doesn't matter what I do, it's not working out, it's hard, it's painful, it's confusing, it's_______ (you fill it in)." It may just be God and His green thumb at work in your life.

Mrs. Dea Irby

Dear Precious Vine Dresser, thank you for caring enough to prune me. Help me to yield to your shears. Amen

VERB Check

I will exalt you, my God the King. Psalm 145:1a NIV

What glorious truths about our God can be seen in Psalm 145 through the verbs used! First, note all the truths the "being verb" **is** reveals: the LORD **is** great and worthy ofpraise (v. 3), gracious and compassionate, slow to anger, rich in love (v. 8), good (v. 9), faithful and loving (v. 13b & 17b), righteous (v. 17a), near (v. 18). Did you notice that these truths are presented in the present tense form? Our Lord is, (not was). Choose one of these facts and rest in its implications for you in today's demands. God **is** great: Do you see His majesty in His Creations—-even in that bird landing on your window ledge? Since He has planned His Works so well, will you trust and praise Him today?

Next, find all the "action verbs" that show God's doings, such as He has compassion (v. 9), upholds and lifts up (v. 14), gives food (v. 15). Find the other ones David named and be encouraged!Will you trust Him to uphold you as you face temptations or discouragement? Will you trust Him to provide every need—financially, physically, and spiritually—for you, your family, and your friends? Let's not forget the responses that David declares should come from our hearts and lives—exaltation and praise (v. 1), commendation (v. 4), proclamation (v. 6), celebration (v. 7)!Find others on which to meditate and take action. Sing while mopping the kitchen floor. Tell a neighbor how Jesus has met a need. Worship regularly with believers. If you ever have a hard time exalting or commending our Lord, start back at Calvary!

MRS. CAROLYN LYON

My God the King, I praise You for allowing me to know this rich fellowship with You! Amen

Heroes

Search me, O God, and know my heart; test me and know my anxious thoughts. See if there is any offensive way in me, and lead me in the way everlasting. Psalm 139:23-24 NIV

Busy day. Tired feet. The comfy couch offered brief relief. I flipped on the TV, looking for a few minutes of lighthearted entertainment. Instead, images of celebrities, ambitious people, and get-rich-quick schemes filled the channels. Grab for more, claw your way to the top, I was instructed. Be successful!

David had to wrestle with these same issues—he was a king, for goodness' sake. And he was human. It's encouraging to have his earnest prayer written down for me to read and follow suit. The same God he walked with is available and desires to guide me. He wants to define purpose and success for each of us. I must seek after Him daily, giving him my dreams, ambitions, and allegiance. Although I fall flat on my face constantly, I pray that I'll pursue Him and his desires for me more passionately than anything I want on earth. People who live this way consistently are real-life heroes to me, and hopefully for all of us.

MRS. ALISON BRYANT

Father, thank you that You know my heart and give me purpose. Help me to follow your desires for my life. Amen

Guidelines and Signposts

In all thy ways acknowledge him, and he shall direct thy paths.
Proverbs 3:6 KJV

I am fascinated with funny names of streets and towns. We were in a shop looking at some photographs of signs from towns and cities across North Carolina. As we talked with the owner of the shop, he stated that he had been to all the little towns in our state and taken pictures of unusual road and town signs. We asked if he had seen the sign "Buzzards Crossroads." He said he had and quickly showed us the sign. We had to buy this for a friend who always said as we were in a large city with all the traffic: "I would rather be in Buzzards Crossroads!" (I don't know why anyone would want to be because there is nothing there but a stop sign.) I also read that in Shelby, North Carolina, there are two street signs: "Betta Way" and "Thissa Way."

We need signs, maps, and guides as we travel to avoid becoming lost. When I travel, I use OnStar on my car—it has helped me many times. But for Christian living, there is only One reliable guide. He has given clear guidelines for our lives in the Bible, but not many follow them today. Nevertheless, God promises that if we acknowledge Him and follow His guidelines, He will direct our paths. And you can be sure that His way is the "Betta Way."

Mrs. Betsy McSwain

Lord, help us to follow the guidelines in your Word. Amen

Where Pigs DO Fly

Every good and perfect gift is from above... James 1:17a NIV

There it goes again. With snorts and buzzes, one pink plastic pig soars through the room, propelled by our youngest son's hand. A son we never imagined we would have. A few years ago, Bruce and I thought our family was complete with Jason, almost a teenager, and younger brothers, Brian and baby Benjamin. But my surprise fortieth birthday present would come eight years later. Thoughts of Abraham and Sarah came to mind, as we questioned God's wisdom. As the months passed, our sons observed how a mother carries a burden but considers it a blessing. My expanding silhouette became the topic of serious conversations. "Mom, is that a basketball under your shirt?" and "Well, then, I have a kitty in MY tummy!"

I celebrated my milestone birthday with eight hours of false labor. Nine days later, we welcomed Joseph Sterling. Our hearts melted. His brothers experienced a new dynamic in brotherhood. I treasured the bond of another nursing baby. Shortly after weaning, Joseph patted my chest and sighed, "Milky went bye-bye. Mommy broken. Two brokens." (He likes to count.) Life passes quickly. These precious moments can get lost in the shuffle. But for now, pigs can once again fly. Geckos are bathed, while dinosaurs play in barns next to cows, horses, AND Superman. Precious quotes are being recorded. There is joy in teaching another wee one that "Yes, Jesus loves you." The Lord has answered our prayers by handing us the puzzle piece we didn't know was missing. We are even better equipped to serve Jesus, who gives every perfect gift.

Mrs. Margie Campbell

Lord, help me trust that the threads woven into my life are chosen by the Master Designer. Amen

Gone Fishing

Then He said to them, "Follow Me, and I will make you fishers of men."
Matthew 4:19 NKJ

I love this remarkable story in Matthew 4: 18-22. Jesus, walking by the Sea of Galilee, in a matter of moments, changes the lives of four fishermen and the history of the world. We don't know how many other fishermen there were on the shore that day, but there are a few words here that I don't think are accidental. Simon and Andrew were throwing a dragnet into the sea when He called them. The scriptures say "At once they left their nets. . . ."Nets were not only expensive to buy but were extremely time-consuming to make. They left them. Maybe they knew no one would bother them. I don't know, but I'm impressed that they simply "left their nets" without folding them up, without hiding them under a boat, without making sure their means of making a living was taken care of. And then, Jesus walked a bit further and called to James and John who were in the boat with their father, mending nets. They were busy at work doing what had to be done if they were going to successfully catch fish. Nets with holes lose fish. All four men were busy as fishermen. All four left their work, their means of financial security, their hard-earned security. They left it all to follow Him without a discussion about possible benefits. James and John even left their father to do all the work.

Years later, we find Peter and Andrew active in evangelism—a fishing of another kind. Only this time they are catching men. And James and John continued to "mend nets," making sure the emerging Church was discipled in truth and that fledging Christians understood the Truth.

Mrs. Jackie Sheppard

Lord, in my busy life, may I never be too busy to leave all and follow You. Amen

Divine Interruptions

In all your ways acknowledge Him, and He will make your paths straight. Proverbs 3:6 NASB

I almost missed God the other day. It had been a particularly busy day. One of those days where the "to do" list could easily have filled my entire weekly calendar. Late in the afternoon, my phone rang. The receptionist announced that I had a guest. Glancing at my calendar, I realized that I had no appointment scheduled. Slightly annoyed at the interruption, I went to the lobby to greet my unexpected guest. Waiting there was a young woman and her teenage daughter. "I am sorry that I came without an appointment," the young woman began. "I have been trying to get enough courage to come see you for several weeks. Could I have just a few minutes of your time?" Once in my office, she began to unfold her story. Six months earlier, her husband had been brutally murdered, an unsolved crime with the trail growing cold. A believer, all she wanted to hear was that God really did have a purpose for her life. After spending a few minutes talking about her goals and mapping a course for the next few months, we prayed, hugged, and they left.

My guest came thinking that she needed to see me when, in fact, I really needed to see her. I needed to be reminded of the blessings of God-interruptions. Marilyn Hontz wrote these challenging words, "Invite God to interrupt you. If your heavenly Father wanted to, could He interrupt you at any time during the day to ask you to do something with Him?" Invite God to interrupt you today. You have no idea what kind of blessing or adventure awaits you.

MRS. DAYNA STREET

Lord, arrange my day according to your agenda, not mine. Amen

Who Is It?

> *For it is by grace you have been saved, through faith–and this not from yourselves, it is the gift of God.* Ephesians 2:8 NIV

In the last six months my husband has been sick twice with the stomach flu, both times after church on Sunday. On these two occasions women came to our door asking for money. It is not hard to find our house because we live in the parsonage on church property. The first woman I had never met before; her boyfriend sent her to ask for gas money. I proceeded to explain that my husband was sick and that I could not help her. After a short discussion she left without any gas money. She was probably angry. I was definitely angry about being bothered. I was tired and this was not my "area." My husband is much better at handling people.

The second time the doorbell rang, I recognized the woman standing in the doorway with her little girl. We had helped her two other times. This time she needed money for groceries. I let her know that my husband was sick and that he could possibly call her in the morning. But that was not soon enough for her. When I offered her groceries from my kitchen, she agreed and I invited her in. Upon receiving the groceries she thanked me and left. I started to get frustrated, remembering the same situation the last time my husband was sick. Instead of letting my frustration turn into anger, that time I stopped and asked the Lord if He was sending these women to my house to remind me how much we all need gracious help.

Mrs. Krissy Guhl

> *Lord God, soften my heart to those you put in my life. In Jesus' Name. Amen*

Don't Miss It!

The sons of Ephraim were archers equipped with bows, yet they turned back in the day of battle...They forgot His deeds and His miracles that He had shown them. Psalm 78:9, 11 NASB

"Help me Obie Wan Konobie, you're my only hope." In the movie, *Star Wars*, Obie Wan has been living as a hermit on the back side of a barren planet while war was being waged by Darth Vader against everyone in the galaxy. Watching this movie, I couldn't help but wonder: "Obie Wan, what in the world are you doing? You're a Jedi Knight! They need you and you're hanging out in a cave?" It made no sense to me that he wasn't in the thick of the battle when so much was at stake. But, frankly, as I write this more than 30 years later, I have to admit I understand old Obie Wan a little better. Because we are in a war too, aren't we? There is a spiritual battle being waged for the hearts and minds of all of us. These battles frequently center on personal challenges or weariness in ministry. And more often than I care to admit, there are times when I wouldn't mind escaping to the back side of a barren planet.

In today's Scripture, the sons of Ephraim were trained archers and yet, they turned back when the battle began. Why? They forgot God's deeds and His miracles. It is so easy to get our eyes on the problems and not on Him–the Creator of the universe who lives in us, forgetting that He is equipping us for our own special life of service.

Mrs. Danelle Nelson

Lord, help me to see YOU and live the joyful life you want me to have. YOU are my only hope! Amen

The Good Side of Anger?

On reaching Jerusalem, Jesus entered the temple area and began driving out those who were buying and selling there. He overturned the tables of the money changers and the benches of those selling doves, and would not allow anyone to carry merchandise through the temple courts. Mark 11:15-16 NIV

Our Bible study topic with the youth one Wednesday night was anger. The teenagers responded with candid food for thought. *Can some anger be good?* We discussed it. I chewed on that mental meal for days. We can ask Jesus while He's in the temple courts in Jerusalem right now. But wait, He seems to be busy. Whoa! Watch out for the flying tables and projectile pots. Yes, I'd say that He is angry. Profiteers have set up shop in His father's house of worship, taking advantage of His people. He won't settle for that. Hmm, perhaps anger—when we get angry at the right things—can be fuel for goodness and change.

What crosses your mind (and heart) when you see injustice? When someone is taken advantage of? When corruption poisons the world around you? Our reaction can be anger channeled for good, the motivation to begin to right the wrongs and promote God's love and justice. Perhaps it could motivate us to pray more fervently, to climb into the world of a hurting person, to speak up and fight for God's truth. So, what makes you really angry? A friend who snaps at you or the driver who cuts you off in traffic? Instead of getting angry, may passion for what touches Jesus' heart drive us to act in love.

Mrs. Alison Bryant

Jesus, help me to see today the things that make You angry, turning it into good for your sake. Amen

Mental Multi-tasking

And forgive us our debts, as we also have forgiven our debtors.
Matthew 6:12 NASB

I consider myself a Master at being a jack of all trades!I can do many of those trades at the same time. I've nursed a baby while cooking and talking on the phone and helping a child do homework. I've worked on my computer while watching a football game and listening to music. I know you are probably able to do the same. We have to if we are going to live up to that lady in Proverbs 31!

This "condition" causes a problem sometimes in church. I'm sitting or standing there participating yet my mind is making a list of people to talk with after service or planning what to do for dinner. Typically I get away with this (from my perspective only), but one Sunday God spoke loud and clear. My mind had wandered off to my business. I needed to expand my shelving and storage at my tearoom. I didn't have any money in my budget for it. Who did I know who would be able to help me if I bought the supplies? Oh, I know. Mr. "Unidentified." He is a builder and fully capable. And, I continued to reason, after what happened with him and my family, he owes us. He should do this for free. As I was thinking these thoughts, I was standing reciting the Lord's Prayer and came to the portion, "and forgive us our debts, as we also have forgiven our debtors." Oh, God, I am so sorry! I was struck with deep conviction. And I certainly didn't want God to forgive me as I was (actually wasn't) forgiving Mr. "Unidentified." I praise God that He disciplines me and purifies my heart!

Mrs. Dea Irby

Lord, reveal to me my sinful un-forgiveness and help me to love with your love. Amen

El Shaddai

And my God shall supply all your need according to His riches in glory by Christ Jesus. Philippians 4:19 NKJ

Down through the years God has so faithfully supplied the needs of our family of five children. Once when our first child was a tiny baby, we had a period of financial difficulties and had no money for baby food and other things. What would we do to feed our little baby girl? That Sunday when we returned from church, there was a bag of baby food at the door with twenty-five dollars in cash in the bag. That was a lot of money in the early sixties. And the baby food was the exact brand and kind that I had started her on. To this day we do not know whom God used to provide that need of ours. We thank God for being so merciful to us.

God has done so many things like this throughout our forty-eight years of ministry. When we faithfully serve Him, He does supply every thing we need—though not necessarily everything we want. But sometimes He even gives us non-necessities that we would like. Hallelujah! What a mighty God we serve. He is El Shaddai, the God who provides more than we could ever ask or think.

MRS. BETTY MICK

Thank you, Lord, for so faithfully and mercifully providing our needs, and then some. As we serve you, Lord, help us to be examples of your greatness. Amen

Unlikely Ministry Tools

So the LORD said to him, "What is that in your hand?"
Exodus 4:2 NKJ

When a hijacked plane hit Tower One of the World Trade Center on September 11, 2001, the power failed. Jan Demczur, a window washer, became trapped on an elevator on the 50th floor with five other men, mostly executives. While the men discussed what to do, Demczur began prying open the elevator doors with the handle of his squeegee. Others helped him until the doors yielded. The elevator, however, was an express with no opening on the 50th floor. Again Demczur considered his assets. Using the sharp edge of his squeegee, he began scraping at the wall. The men took turns scratching through three layers of dry wall, creating a hole big enough for their escape. The six men survived because one of them, an unlikely hero, simply used what he already had at hand.

When Moses balked at the task God ordained for him, his ordinary shepherd's staff became a miracle-working emblem of God's presence and power. Because Moses used what was in his hand, God rescued a whole nation from bondage. What is at hand for me to use for God's work? An extra bedroom for traveling missionaries? A computer to type letters for my husband or send encouraging e-mails? A butter knife to make sandwiches for the homeless? Car keys to drive a widow to the doctor? Like Jan Demczur, we can look for ways to use the resources and abilities we already have. God expects no more and no less.

MRS. MARCIA HORNOK

Lord, help me to discern people's needs and be quick to offer my helping hands. Amen

"Oh, no, I have P. K. s!"

I will walk within my house in the integrity of my heart.
Psalm 101:2b NASB

My husband and I were married between first and second semester in seminary while I did field work for my Christian Education degree. Six months later we learned our tribe was increasing. Then it dawned on us that our precious little bundle would be a P. K. just like all the other seminary students' children. We began to ask many questions. Why is that a bad thing? Why are "preacher's kids" so stereotyped? How can one rear them outside the box of expectations?

My husband and I have studied the phenomenon of children in the ministry and have considered a few options. These are perhaps a few reasons some "P. K."s rebel: 1) pressure to perform, hearing "what will people think?"; 2) neglect, the church is put before the family; 3)exclusion from ministering, not sharing the vision; 4) feeling in competition with God; and possibly the strongest cause 5) hypocrisy, inconsistency. You can fool some of the people all the time and all of the people some of the time, but you can't fool children! If Dad stands before the congregation and proclaims God's Word but doesn't live it in the home or Mom is an angel at church but a demon at home, a child will see the inconsistency. Doubt in the truth follows doubt in the source of truth (parents). The reality of Christianity comes into question. Scripture teaches us to walk within our homes with integrity. That includes being honest about who we are and who God is. Yes, parents are sinners who need to repent and apologize when necessary. (It's not like the children don't know we are wrong.) Confession is not only good for the soul, it is good for the health of the family.

MRS. DEA IRBY

Lord, help me to walk within my house with integrity. Amen

Autumn Displays God's Splendor

Worship the Lord in the splendor of his holiness...

Psalm 96:9 NIV

Driving through our area just northeast of Memphis, Tennessee, during the autumn, causes me to sing out praise to our God the creator. The wonder of all the different trees that God gives us to enjoy during the spring and the summer now burst out in splendor and majesty. The brilliant lemon yellows blend with golden tones, while the rich crimson reds coordinate with the spicy oranges. I am consistently amazed at the details that God shows us to remind His children that He cares deeply for us. He is waiting for us to look upward and enjoy this wonderful display of His splendor. Psalm 96 tell us in verse 1, "Sing to the Lord a new song; sing to the Lord all the earth." Driving to church there is a road where the trees actually make a canopy, giving a tunnel effect. The glorious colors of the trees on this road remind me to sing out praise to Him as the Protector of my soul. Did you know that even the trees sing out? Verse 12b says, "Then all the trees of the forest will sing for joy." Read these verses and commit them to memory.

When dealing with difficult people or situations, or when you do not understand what God is trying to teach you, remind yourself of the splendor of the trees. We do not understand how the trees change their colors, but God does. He knows the time table and He wants us to burst out in song because He reigns. He will reveal the path you need to follow.

Mrs. Shirley J. Ellis

Sing to the Lord who reveals His majesty to us. Amen

Who Me?

Now therefore go, and I will be with thy mouth, and teach thee what thou shalt say. Exodus 4:12 KJV

The first time God revealed His personal name **Yahweh** in Scripture was to Moses. God had reminded Moses of the covenant He made with Israel and how He would fulfill His promise. As God was instructing Moses for a special task, Moses immediately began making excuses, such as his lack of ability and eloquence of speech. However, God had an answer for all his objections. Many Christians are able to relate to Moses' resistance to God's calling. God does not ask us to be what we are not, rather He only asks us to yield what we are to Him.

FOOD FOR THOUGHT: 1) God appeared to Abraham, Isaac and Jacob, as El Shaddai or God Almighty (Exodus 6:3), but to Moses He used His personal covenant name translated LORD. 2) Reflect on the above Scripture readings and make a list of Moses' excuses and God's responses (cf. Philippians 4:13 and 1 Corinthians 2:1-5). 3) God allowed Moses to take along his brother Aaron as a source of encouragement and support (cf. Luke 10:1). 4) Why does God call one person to become a leader while allowing another to live an obscure life? Is our future determined by our ability or God's sovereignty? 5) Moses was a prince who became a shepherd; David, a shepherd who became a king. God knows how to prepare each of us to fulfill His plan. If we focus on our limitations, serving the Lord may seem impossible. However, God will enable us to accomplish His mission.

Mrs. Lori Ciccanti

Father, your grace is sufficient and your strength is made perfect in our weakness. Amen

The King and I

A lizard can be caught with the hand, yet it is found in kings' palaces.
Proverbs 30:28 NIV

I know what you're thinking. That this is the weirdest verse you've ever seen at the top of a devotional! Yes, it is weird, but it is in the Bible. I've read through Proverbs many times, so this verse came to mind quickly when the occasion came along to see it in action. After living in Ukraine for ten years, I finally made it down to Crimea, the part of the country that's on the beautiful Black Sea. As we were touring the grounds of a palace, guess what I saw scurrying around? Yes, a lizard! I immediately thought of this verse. Then I began to think about the context of the verse and what Solomon was saying. Solomon was giving examples of some tiny, insignificant creatures that don't seem like they're very important in the world's eyes, but they made it in the Bible. The character displayed by these creatures may not be noticed by many, but the wisest man who ever lived took notice and wants us to do the same.

You may not view yourself as very wise or important to the world. Maybe you think you're at the bottom of the food chain like the lizard. But you're not. You've been made in God's image, and you're a part of a king's kingdom. Not only are you a part of His kingdom, you have access to His palace. Better yet, His throne! And you don't have to slip past the guards to get there.

Mrs. Kenyon Powers

Lord, give me wisdom as I live and work for your kingdom. Amen

The Alphabet Song

…"I am the Alpha and the Omega, the Beginning and the End."
Revelation 21:6 NIV

While looking up a word in the dictionary, have you ever found yourself humming the alphabet as you learned it as a child? It's interesting to know that no matter how long and complicated an English word might be, the 26 letters of our alphabet are sufficient for its spelling! I find it interesting that the Holy Spirit had John record "The Greek Alphabet Song" several times for encouragement to the early churches and to us. In Revelation 1:8 he writes, "'I am the Alpha (first letter of the Greek alphabet) and the Omega' ([last letter), says the Lord God, 'who is, and who was, and who is to come, the Almighty.'" In the Revelation 21 description of the New Jerusalem, John quotes the One seated on the throne as saying, "It is done. I am the Alpha and the Omega, the Beginning and the End."A third time this song is sung in Revelation 22:13.

How reassuring it is to know that our Lord Jesus Christ is all we need in living today, tomorrow, and right into eternity! One of our Bible professors at Columbia International University would often challenge and encourage us by saying, "Remember, young people, our God is our A, our B, our C, and all the way to our Z. He is ALL we need!" Because He is all we need, can we not trust our lives, our loved ones, our needs, and our works into His loving care?

MRS. CAROLYN LYON

Thank You, Lord that you are indeed all I need!Help my life spell out this truth to others. Amen

Best Friends

But there is a friend who sticks closer than a brother.
Proverbs 18:24b NASB

When my daughter was nine years old, God called her to international missions. At that time my husband was the pastor of a small mission church meeting in an elementary school. There were no other children in our daughter's grade at the church. I prayed daily for God to send a family to our church with a girl who would become a good friend to our daughter. I dreamed of them attending school together, sleeping over at each others' house, having the same standards and morals as our family. As time went on, I questioned why God would not grant my request. I knew God loved my daughter more than even I did, so I could not understand why He would deny my child a best friend. I kept on praying.

After almost two years of earnestly praying for my child, God reminded me He knew what was best for her. He gently pointed out that as a missionary in another country there would be many lonely days. He was preparing a child to know how to handle being lonely. He was teaching her to depend on her relationship with Him in all circumstances. He was teaching her that Jesus is a friend who sticks closer than a brother. Our daughter is now in college, six hundred miles from home, preparing for missions. She will spend this summer in Romania serving our Lord. I am so thankful that God has taught her to depend on Him even when she feels all alone.

Mrs. Karen A. Dishman

Thank you God for doing what is best for my child. Even when I don't understand, help me to trust You completely. Amen

Don't Be Caught Sleeping

Then he [Jesus] returned to his disciples and found them sleeping. "Could you men not keep watch with me for one hour?" he asked Peter. "Watch and pray so that you will not fall into temptation. The spirit is willing, but the body is weak."

Matthew 26:40-41 NIV

Recently I was reading about the events leading up to the passion of Christ. Jesus' conversation with his disciples in the garden of Gethsemane stood out to me like never before—perhaps because I actually visited that garden in Israel last fall. Jesus wanted the disciples to stay awake and pray with Him, but they kept falling asleep. He was trying to prepare them for the trial that was coming. "Don't sleep, pray!" was His instruction. He knew they were going to be tempted beyond what they could bear if they didn't talk to God in earnest. But the disciples didn't pray—they slept—demonstrating the weakness of their flesh.

How well I know that feeling! Often as I work alongside my husband in ministry, my spirit is willing to do what is right, but my body and mind are weary and just do not want to participate. If I don't stay in close contact with God through prayer, my flesh can easily take over and rule (or ruin) my day. Does that ever happen to you? If so, pray with me the prayer below.

Mrs. Helen Krudop

Precious Lord, often my flesh is tired, and I just don't feel like spending time with You. Forgive me and draw me to You in quiet conversation so that I might face what comes tomorrow. Amen

Forgiveness

Let all bitterness, and wrath, and anger, and clamour, and evil speaking, be put away from you, with all malice: And be ye kind one to another, tenderhearted, forgiving one another, even as God for Christ's sake hath forgiven you. Ephesians 4:31-32 KJV

So let me get this straight. I am to be kind, tenderhearted, and forgiving even when I am being attacked or my family is being attacked? Why? Because, Jesus was! As a pastor's wife, I am under the watchful eye of the congregation at all times. I find myself a little more tolerant of attacks against myself and even my husband, but when our children are under attack, I find myself becoming a Mama bear protecting her cubs.

And it is not just my own children that are sometimes attacked, it's all the teens and children in our church. I believe we need to protect our children the best we can from being taken advantage of and from verbal abuse within the church. But we do need to do it kindly, tenderheartedly, and with forgiveness for those who would abuse them. There seems to be so much un-forgiveness in the church today. We need to set the right example for others. Will it be easy? I don't think so! I can't imagine it was easy for Jesus to ask His Father to forgive those who crucified Him as He was hanging on the cross. Maybe if we keep that in mind, it will help us be more like Him.

Mrs. Bonnie M. Lambert

Help me, Lord, to be more like Jesus, kind, tenderhearted, and forgiving of my brothers and sisters. Amen

Fighting Discouragement

.... Be strong and courageous, and do the work. Do not be afraid or discouraged, for the LORD God, my God is with you. . .
I Chronicles 28:20 NIV

Remember in the movie "It's a Wonderful Life" where God is giving Clarence the angel his assignment, George Bailey. The angel asked "What's wrong with him; is he sick?" God replied "No! Worse, he's discouraged!" How often do you find yourself as a pastor's wife, fighting discouragement? When you're in full-time ministry and involved in so many people's lives, I know you are sometimes in this battle. Satan is ready for any opportunity to discourage you. Should we be surprised at this? No! The Bible warns us that Satan is prowling around wanting to steal and destroy.

Being discouraged is a feeling of hopelessness, of losing faith in what you have hoped for. Discouragement attacks our faith. When all of a sudden things have changed and you doubt yourself or what God is doing, ask yourself, "What is God trying to teach me?" He may have different and better plans for us, if we'll let Him teach us through the discouraging times of our lives. There are many things that can discourage us: a struggle in our life that we see as a losing battle, difficulties in relationships, ministry problems or being misunderstood. Living in Ukraine these past ten years has added a new twist to discouragement because of the language and cultural barriers. I believe true suffering is when God allows things in your life that only He can work out for your good (not you coming to your own rescue).

Mrs. Kenyon Powers

God, as You encourage me, help me to be an encouragement to others. Amen

Louder than Words

Only conduct yourselves in a manner worthy of the gospel of Christ.... Philippians 1:27a NASB

Many of us are familiar with the cliché, "Your actions are speaking so loud, I can't hear what you're saying!" As followers of the Lord Jesus Christ, we should have actions that are representative of what we are saying. If I tell my husband that I love him but shun him when he speaks to me or pull away from him when he touches me, does he feel love from me? Do I really love him? It's sobering to think that we can say one thing and show something completely different with our actions or attitudes. Think of this situation: A child is asked to straighten up his bedroom before going out to play. He immediately asks, "Oh, Mommy, do I have to?" The mother explains that he needs to take care of responsibilities before getting to have privileges. The child hangs his head, drags his feet, and draws out his words as he says, "Yes Mommy." He may be using the right words, but his unwilling heart is evident.

We may struggle in this same way in our walk with the Lord. Maybe we tell Him that we are so grateful for all He has done. Then almost in the next breath, we complain about our circumstances and show discontentment. If we want our life to exemplify the work of the Holy Spirit in us, we need to take a close look at our heart. Do people see Christ when they interact with us? Or do our actions speak so loudly that they can't hear the gospel?

MRS. VICKI WOODS

Heavenly Father, let my heart be more and more genuinely in love with You so that my words and actions would convey Your truth to the world around me. Amen

Go Team!

> *Two are better than one, because they have a good reward for their toil.* Ecclesiastes 4:9 ESV

For my bridal shower, one of the gifts I received was a football. It was a symbol of my husband's and my friendship. When we first got married, we threw the football all the time, scrimmaging with one another. We played basketball together, went running together…I even called him "Coach" at times. Ministry was much the same. We were inseparable. We were together for church visits, hospital visits, associational meetings, Bible studies…and then we had kids! Suddenly, our "team" was very different. I was staying home on visitation night. He visited at the hospital alone. Associational meetings without nursery were torture and Bible studies were out of the question.

I have finally come to realize that God gives us seasons of ministry. Sometimes our ministering seems worlds apart and yet it is all for the Kingdom. Some days I may minister only to my two boys, other days it might include a group of ladies, other days it might be a family coming over for lunch where our whole family may minister together. As my husband's helpmeet, it's my delight always to be ministering to him, making him as successful as possible. We still occasionally throw the football and sometimes shoot hoops together, but even as we minister separately for this season, we are still a team…and the greatest part is that we are always on the winning side!

Mrs. Melody A. Hertler

Father, may my husband and I always be a team. May we minister together for the sake of your Kingdom. Amen

Earning Eternal Rewards

Each of you should look not only to your own interests, but also to the interests of others. Philippians 2:4 NIV

One of the lessons learned from the movie, *Mr. Holland's Opus*, is the importance of investing our life in people rather than pursuing self-fulfilling goals. Mr. Holland's lifelong desire was to write a grand symphony, but to support his family he taught music at a high school. Involvement with students before and after school left little time to work on his symphony. Then after thirty years of devoted teaching, school funds were cut, forcing him to retire. Grieving over this "death" of his dreams and his career, he packed up his classroom for the last time. His wife and son accompanied him and covertly channeled him toward the school auditorium. When he opened the door, the room erupted into applause and cheers as he entered. His former students, fellow teachers, and admiring townspeople had assembled to honor him for all the ways he had touched their lives. He finally realized that these people were his symphony—his life's work.

We may never accomplish our personal dreams or experience a standing ovation on earth, but if we faithfully pour our life into others, perhaps our reception into heaven will be like what Mr. Holland experienced. Along with God's "Well done," it may include our own "great cloud of witnesses" who will give us "a rich welcome into the eternal kingdom of our Lord and Savior Jesus Christ" (2 Peter 1:11 NIV).

MRS. MARCIA HORNOK

Wean me from selfish ambitions, which are temporal, and give me opportunities to invest my life in people, who are eternal. Amen

Enjoy Your Husband

Wives, in the same way be submissive to your husbands so that, if any of them do not believe the word, they may be won over without words by the behavior of their wives, when they see the purity and reverence of your lives. I Peter 3:1-2 NIV

One definition of "reverence" in this passage of Scripture, is to "enjoy your husband." The person who taught me about "enjoying my husband" was a humble pastor's wife named Gannel Stone. Her husband was a country church preacher. He did carpentry work or plowed fields for the farmers in his church to supplement their income. Their lives were simple and, at times, meager. I observed many things about this lady and the way she treated her husband. She did the "spiritual things" like submission, respect, and honor. She appreciated and was devoted to him. She praised him a lot. It was evident that she was deeply in love with him. But the practical thing she modeled for me was how she enjoyed her husband. He was her hero. She laughed at his humor, cultivated inside jokes, encouraged his dreams, and cheerfully supported the ministry to which God called him. I'm sure at times it required a choice on her part—just as it will require a choice on ours.

One of my life goals was to teach my daughters to love their husbands as I have tried to love their dad for the past 37 years because of the example modeled for my by this sweet pastor's wife. Gannel Stone was my mentor. Oh, did I mention that she was also my dear mother?

Mrs. Vonna S. Downs

Lord, teach us to be not only in love with our husbands, but to honor them with devotion. Amen

Just Ask

Ask and it will be given to you; seek and you will find. . .
Matthew 7:7 NIV

I remember reading an article about a missionary who left Africa very disappointed because all the years that she had lived there no one had invited her to a meal in their home while she had invited many Africans to eat in her home. The main point of this article was that the missionary didn't know the African mode of hospitality. If she had only understood that Africans didn't invite you to come for a meal; they just felt honored if you simply showed up to eat attheir home uninvited. If the missionary had known this about the African culture she would have had a totally different perspective on how she was accepted.

This story made me think of the times I have felt neglected, unappreciated, and taken for granted by my husband. The truth is many times I feel this way is because I have not seen situations from his perspective. To understand my husband's perspective, I need to ask questions about how he is thinking and feeling. When I come across as loving and respectful, my questions are more prone to heighten romance because a man needs respect like he needs air to breathe. This is the way God designed him. A man can easily love a woman who treats him with respect. Just think what a different feeling the missionary we read about at the beginning of this devotional would have had if she had only asked a few questions. May our days be filled with many loving questions as we seek to tenderly understand our mates' perspective.

Mrs. Janice Upton

Dear Jesus, when my spouse does things I don't understand, help me to gently ask questions. Amen

Of All Comfort

...My grace is sufficient for thee 2 Corinthians 12:9 KJV ...the God of all comfort. II Corinthians 1:3 KJV

Two things I learned on the night of September 17, 1980. God's grace is sufficient, and He is the Father of all comfort. Our son Matthew was born prematurely. As I held his little, lifeless body, I thought my heart would break and perhaps physically explode. Many of you have felt that kind of pain. My husband was grieving himself but was trying his best to be strong and comfort me. But you can not truly comfort someone when you can't feel the depth of her pain. He was sad, but as a mother, I had already started a deep love affair with this baby, felt him grow, and felt him move. No one could know the depth of grief I was experiencing except Jesus. Some things you can only learn through great sorrow. This was such a time. I learned that His promise is true. His grace IS sufficient whether you accept it or not. It is up to you whether you take advantage of His amazing offer.

The other truth I learned when I climbed up in His lap, let Him put His arms around me and rock me to that place of peace and comfort that only He knows how to reach. He IS the Father of all comfort. He did for me what a wise person once told me was possible: sometimes God will allow a tear in your eye so He can put a new song in your heart.

Mrs. Vonna S. Downs

Father of grace and comfort, show us how to accept your promises. Amen

Children in the Church

And they brought young children to him, that he should touch them: and his disciples rebuked those that brought them. But when Jesus saw it, he was much displeased, and said unto them, Suffer the little children to come unto me, and forbid them not: for of such is the kingdom of God. Mark 10:13-14 KJV

The Lord has given me a gift to work in children's ministry. I know how very important children are to Him. Jesus was "much displeased" when the disciples tried to stop people from bringing children to Him. Should we be any less displeased by the congregational members that consider the children of the church to be liabilities? As a mother, it breaks my heart to see how prevalent this attitude is in some of our churches.

We need to remember that the children are the church's greatest assets. In five to ten years the teens of the church will be our new leaders, in fifteen to twenty years the elementary school children will be, and in twenty-five to thirty years the babies will be leading the church. Without children learning and growing in our church, the church will die. We need to encourage the children to participate in the church services, have the teens lead the worship at least once a month, have the children's church sing once a month. There are so many ways to get the children involved with the church services and to get the congregation to see them becoming part of the church. Children are very important to Jesus, and we must not hinder them from coming to Him.

MRS. BONNIE M. LAMBERT

Help us to remember how important children are to You and help us to be compassionate, accepting, and loving to all those that You bring to our church. In Jesus' name. Amen

TRUST (Part I)

But he who trusts in the LORD, lovingkindness shall surround him. Psalm 32:10b NASB

I gently set the phone back on its cradle, but inwardly I slammed it down. I turned, quickly walking out of the room so that my sons wouldn't see the tears welling up in my eyes. My husband of thirty years was halfway around the world from me, and I had wanted nothing more than to talk to him. To have a simple heart-to-heart conversation. He was on his dream trip-of-a-lifetime: a five-week study tour in Israel. My hearing loss had prevented any good communication for weeks. Opportunities for e-mailing were sparse. Our phone calls were reduced to me talking and then waiting for one of our sons to translate Bruce's responses to me. The phone passed back and forth between us. Real personal! It was a warm, humid Hawaiian day. My hearing aids had built up moisture, causing voices to sound especially crackly. I snatched the aids off my ears, tossed them into the dehumidifier, and ran to the back yard. The hose mimicked the tears streaming down my face, as I aimed it at my sweet peas. Their sweet scent wafted back to me, which on most days, would have brought me joy. But today my anger was vented at God as I shouted in my mind, "WHERE ARE YOU IN ALL OF THIS?"

"Don't you trust me? "I turned to see the man whose voice I'd heard. But no one was there. Then it dawned on me. I'd taken out my hearing aids. I was standing in my silent world. Again I heard, "Don't you trust ME?" Did I trust God? Do you in times like these?

[To be continued in the next devotional]

MRS. MARGIE CAMPBELL

From the depth of my soul I cry out to You, Lord, to make sense of life. Amen

TRUST (Part II)

Trust in Him at all times . . . pour out your heart before Him.
Psalm 62:8 NASB

Shocked at the clarity of God's voice as I stood in my yard, I said, "Yes, Lord, I trust You. I just don't understand why everything I love is being taken away . . . music, worship, children's ministry. Even simple conversations are difficult. Being a pastor's wife without hearing seems equivalent to requiring the Israelites to make more bricks without providing the straw! Are you taking everything away because I wasn't doing it well enough?" I'd slipped into my usual mode of feeling inadequate.

He replied, ever so gently, "It's not that at all, Margie. I have something different for you to do." I was shocked again. I'd never thought that He could use my hearing loss to redirect my life. It's felt like such a heavy anchor. *Heal me quick, Lord, so I can get on with living for You! :)* How many of us feel that way though? We want the hardships of life to go away so we can be more fully used by Him. Sometimes He literally has to quiet our world, so He can show us a different plan, one that will bring glory to His holy name. I've since had to deal with other tragedies of life—losing my father and our childhood home to a fire and having our youngest son develop diabetes. But each time now, I hear Him whispering, "I have something different for you." I can take another step towards trusting the One who gave His life to save mine. And I praise Him as I take each step.

MRS. MARGIE CAMPBELL

Lord, help me to cease striving and KNOW that you are God. Amen

An Education in Trust

> *Trust in the LORD with all your heart and lean not on your own understanding; in all your ways acknowledge Him and He will make your paths straight.* Proverbs 3:5-6 NIV

"Have you thought about going back to school to get a skill just in case something happens to me so you will be able to support yourself and the kids?" I can hear these words spoken by my husband as if it were yesterday. We had only been at our first pastorate a few years and I was still the mother of three young children. My answer was that I would love to go back to school someday, but right now I am too busy raising little ones. It wasn't long before I was being encouraged by my husband and supportive friends that now was the time to start college to get my teaching degree. My husband was happy to babysit our children. The Lord opened doors and the finances were provided for me to go, so I had no excuses left. The only problem I had were my fears within: "Would I be able to pass or would I fail?" With many questions flooding my mind, all I could hear deep down in my soul was "Trust Me."

When the day came that I marched across the stage to get my teaching degree, my heart was filled with praise because the Lord had been faithful all the way. All those times I felt I could not write another paper, He was there to give me the words I needed. This was His degree to be used for His glory, and He alone was worthy of all the praise.

MRS. JANICE UPTON

> *Dear Jesus, please help me never to say no to you when I feel something is impossible. Amen*

An Audience of One

.... We must obey God rather than men! Acts 5:29 NIV

In a theater production, professional actors are on stage to perform for expectant onlookers with a stage manager perhaps off stage encouraging their efforts. In the ministry, "professional Christians" (also known as church staff and their families) are often on stage to perform for the congregation with God in the wings encouraging. Will there be a standing ovation? Will the reviews be good or bad? This fear of the reviews was very strong as we moved to our new church. At that time, we had four children ages two, four, six and eight. To welcome the new pastor and his family, the church had prepared a reception. Our most gregarious four-year-old son was flitting around meeting and greeting. In his frenzy, he spilled his red punch. Very quietly, but with fervor he determined to clean it up. A mother should be so proud.... if he had not grabbed someone's WHITE crocheted shawl!Aaarrrrgggg!What will people think? It was within the first few Sundays that our two year-old daughter was found at church without her shoes on. Oh, what will people think of the preacher's family whose children are so disrespectful and uncouth. I was put in my place when I confronted the barefoot culprit. (Remember, she is two.) She innocently looked up at me and said, "But Mom, Moses took his shoes off on holy ground!"

Oh, to have that perspective. Only God's review matters. Only God sits in the audience. The Holy Spirit is in the wings prompting and Jesus is empowering us to act out God's script for our lives. We should live before an audience of ONE.

MRS. DEA IRBY

Lord, forgive me for living for the approval of men and not for You. Amen

Pastor's Wife or Wonder Woman?

But they that wait upon the LORD shall renew their strength; they shall mount up with wings as eagles; they shall run, and not be weary; and they shall walk, and not faint. Isaiah 40:31 KJV

Sometimes I think the congregation expects the pastor's wife to fill all the voids in the church. The pastor's wife can be expected to be a Sunday School teacher, Women's Bible Study teacher, church secretary, janitor, Children's Ministry Director, Vacation Bible School Director, Women's Missionary Director, fill in as sound technician and play the piano. This is all while maintaining a spotless house, perfect children, a well-rested husband and being able to go visiting on a moment's notice. And don't forget that if your husband is the pastor of a small to medium-size church, you are probably expected to work outside the home to help fill the gap in his salary.

I am not Wonder Woman. I am a pastor's wife who finds herself clinging to this verse in Isaiah. In the past, I have tried filling most of the roles mentioned above, sometimes all at once. But now I believe that the Lord wants me to look to Him for guidance and direction on which vacancies He wants me to fill (and not just do what I think the congregation expects me to do). If I seek His will for my life, I believe He will honor that by bringing in others to fill the ministry openings. The key is to "wait upon the Lord."

MRS. BONNIE M. LAMBERT

I ask your guidance on which areas of ministry You want me to be involved in. Amen

All My Arrows!

Like arrows in the hands of a warrior are sons born in one's youth. Blessed is the man whose quiver is full of them.

Psalm 127:4-5a NIV

With eight children, I quote this verse and then add, "And I'm quiverful! "We had them in "batches." First, we had a daughter, then two sons, and then another daughter. "That's nice," I thought, "We now have our even family." Life progressed, the children grew and the last was about to start school (YEAH!). For the first time in a decade, I felt like I could get dressed in the morning and still be somewhat presentable that evening. The scent of ammonia had faded. (Oh, by the way, disposable diapers are biblical: "He who **Pampers** his slave from childhood will in the end find him to be a son" Proverbs 29:21. But, the Lord saw fit to bless us with another son. (Actually, we moved and every time we moved, we had a baby.) And another son. And another son. (Affectionately referred to as "The Three Musketeers.") Let's see, isn't seven the biblical number of completion, the perfect number? Well, we moved again and eight years later, on number six's 10th birthday, a precious daughter was added to our quiver.

In case you've lost count, that's three decades of having babies. Whew! With each birth, the first time I was alone with my newborn, I shared two things: 1) you are a precious bundle of sin in need of the Savior Jesus, and 2) if you want to go to college, you will need to get a scholarship! Since then I have prayed three things for each of them: 1) that they would love God with a whole heart; 2) that they would do what is right in His sight; and 3) that they would serve God in a great and mighty way.

Mrs. Dea Irby

Lord, hear my prayers for my arrows and help me be a steadfast archer who glorifies You. Amen

What a Lesson!

But I say to you, love your enemies, bless those who curse you, do good to those who hate you. . . . Matthew 5:44 NKJ

From early childhood, I've been aware of Jesus' command to love our enemies. It never seemed like a problem since generally I got along with everyone. But the words have taken on new meaning over the years of being in ministry with my husband. Of course, we have experienced the blessing of faith growth among our parishioners and have received positive feedback and encouragement from many. But we have also encountered hostility and vicious gossip that cuts to the heart. We recognize them as tools of the enemy intended to destroy our ministry, but that doesn't always make it any easier to turn the other cheek.

Most of the critical remarks are a result of shallow faith and a desire to cling to the traditional roots of a historical church. One gentleman left the church angry because my husband approved the purchase of an artificial Christmas tree, rather than the traditional live cedar tree. Another accused him of preaching "too much from the Bible. "Yet another just didn't like his personality and wanted him removed from the church. Encounters such as these can leave us emotionally and spiritually drained if we don't consciously choose to love these people. We have found that prayer coupled with a decision to love and befriend—in spite of their actions—brings peace to our hearts and can even result in some healed relationships. Consistent love, like a smile, can be contagious!

Mrs. Bonnie M. Lambert

God of relationships, thank you for remarkably teaching me the joy of agape love through the difficult lessons of life. Amen

The Sweet Aroma of Christ

For we are the aroma of Christ to God among those who are being saved and among those who are perishing...

II Corinthians 2:15 ESV

I've watched as tiny seeds grow long stems with buds that open into gorgeous flowers. The fragrance is distinctively different from one flower to the next. In the late summer and early fall, those dying flowers need to be cut back and crushed to prepare the beds for winter. Crushing flowers causes them to yield their most amazing aroma as the flower oils surface, wafting through the air to be enjoyed and appreciated. As my late husband suffered the affects of radiation and chemotherapy that created burns to his body and brought change to his life that many could never imagine, a crushing to who he was as a man, his spirit became sweeter and sweeter. His was a fragrant aroma of a life that so loved the Lord that he was determined to stay focused on Him. Did he struggle? Yes! Did he always *feel* like praising the Lord? No! Was he always satisfied with life that at times seemed to have no purpose? No! However, he was able to draw from the Word of God strength that sustained him, grace in abundance, peace that did pass all understanding, joy unspeakable, and a commitment to be used of God even under the worst of circumstances. His life exuded the sweet aroma of Christ.

Each of us will bloom and our lives will be represented in the early fragrance of our growth. However, the depth of our core foundation will be revealed when crushing (trials) comes and prayerfully, they will reveal the sweet aroma of Christ.

Ms. Patti M. Hummel

Lord, help me to express You in times of ease and especially in times of trial. Amen

Don't Skip Step One

Submit therefore to God, resist the devil and he will flee from you.
James 4:7 NASB

A submitted video on televisions America's Funniest Videos show was of a young wife proudly serving her first turkey at a family gathering. It looked great, but she had skipped step one: take the giblet packet out of the turkey cavity. Well, in her defense, she thought it was prepared stuffing. No real harm was done. But sometimes it is quite detrimental to skip step one.

I was struggling with a mental temptation, mumbling arguments in my mind until I began to counsel myself: "Resist the devil and he will flee from you. Resist the devil and he will flee from you." No matter how sincerely and earnestly I chastised myself, I was getting no relief. "Where is that verse?" I asked. I stopped, looked through my concordance until I found the James 4:7 reference. I turned to it and read, "Submit therefore to God…" Whoa!So that was my problem. I left out the empowering part of the verse. Step One!Then I saw a vision of myself as a little lamb. How often I run to the edge of the pasture and yell at the wolf to go away when I should be hiding behind the Shepherd and asking Him to take care of the wolf. As Peter wrote: "For you were continually straying like sheep, but now you have returned to the Shepherd and Guardian of your souls" (I Peter 2:25 NASB). Don't skip step one: submit to God!

MRS. DEA IRBY

Lord, help me to submit to you to be empowered to overcome temptation. Amen

Yielding

Do you not know that when you present yourselves to someone as slaves for obedience, you are slaves of the one whom you obey, either of sin resulting in death, or of obedience resulting in righteousness? Romans 6:16 NASB

One of the most bizarre experiences we have here in Ukraine is the lack of traffic law enforcement. When there is a high volume of cars at an intersection, it quickly turns to chaos. At these times, it is every man for himself. If an intersection is congested, vehicles simply go around everyone else to be the first in line. This means cars are on the wrong side of the road, on the sidewalks, in the grass, all trying to force their way into the intersection! No one yields to anyone else, and the result is that no one goes anywhere!

God used this traffic situation to speak to me about yielding to Him. The winter months here have been particularly challenging–dark and cold. I have felt the loss of my family and friends more than ever. Just as these drivers felt that their only option was to take things into their own hands and force their way through traffic, I was also taking things into my own hands and not trusting in God's leading, in His sovereignty and His plans, which are always infinitely better than anything that I might come up with. If I don't yield "my way" to "His way," I become a slave to myself and that is not a pretty picture, let me tell you. (My husband can vouch for that!) But if I truly yield myself to Christ, the peace, joy, and rest that I have been seeking flood my soul. May we all yield ourselves to God freshly today, knowing that He wants nothing but His best for us!

Mrs. Danelle Nelson

Lord, help me to yield myself to You, knowing your will is good, acceptable and perfect. Amen

Finishing Well (and Soon)

...but he who holds his tongue is wise. Proverbs 10:19 NIV

On Palm Sunday, my husband's sermon focused on Jesus' words on the cross, "It is finished." The choir also sang the song titled, "It Is Finished." Sitting at the dinner table with our family after the service, I remarked about how beautiful the choir had sounded. "No wonder we gave them spontaneous applause," one son agreed. Another son said, "They should have applauded Dad too for the great sermon." Our daughter quickly added, "Yeah, especially when he said, 'It is finished.' "

We laughed at my daughter's joke, but it made me think. Do I know when to finish talking? Do I monopolize conversations with my interests rather than ask questions to draw others out? When people who are suffering express their grief to me, do I try to "top it" with a story of my own adversity? Trust me—they don't want to hear it! Do I over-stay my welcome on a hospital visit? Fifteen minutes with the patient wanting me to stay is better than thirty with the sick person wishing I would leave. When sharing prayer requests, do I over-explain or suggest ways the problem could be solved? When praying out loud, do I give God all the details (He already knows them, by the way) along with great ideas for how He can answer? Or maybe I "preach" to those in hearing distance, rather than simply talking to God. Brevity is a difficult (but not impossible) discipline for many women because it eliminates our self-focus. No wonder James 1:19 exhorts us to be quick to listen and slow to speak.

MRS. MARCIA HORNOK

Make me sensitive to the need others have to talk, so I will not keep the spotlight shining on myself. Amen

Emphasis

I meditate on your precepts and consider your ways.
Psalm 119:15 NIV

One helpful way to meditate on a truth of God's Word is to emphasis each word separately, noting its application to you.

An example:Hebrews 13:6 "**The** Lord is my Helper….

The **Lord** is my Helper….

The Lord **is** my Helper….

The Lord is **my** Helper….

The Lord is my **Helper**…."

Meditate ("chew your cud") on these truths and then act on them as needed in whatever situation you find yourself today. Remember: God's Word is true no matter how you feel. How about this example:Philippians 4:13 "**I** can do everything through Him….

I **can** do everything through Him….

I can **do** everything through Him….

I can do **everything** through Him….

I can do everything **through** Him….

I can do everything through **Him**…."

MRS. CAROLYN LYON

Lord, please help me place the emphasis correctly today! Amen

My To Do List

For we are His workmanship, created in Christ Jesus for good works, which God prepared beforehand so that we would walk in them. Ephesians 2:10 NASB

"A woman can only do so much!""A pastor's wife can only do so much!""There just aren't enough hours in the day (or night) to get it all done."

I like to pretend there are really twenty-twohours in the day and I've discovered two extra ones!But, that only brings momentary relief. Then I remember this verse in Ephesians. God has prepared my works; I'm to walk in them. Even Jesus did that. At the end of His life, He had not healed every sick person or preached to every person in Israel. In fact, He didn't travel more than a hundred square miles from His hometown. But He could say at the end of His life, "It is finished." He had marked off everything on His to do list. How? God prepared and wrote His to do list. Jesus was in close communication with His Father and knew what He needed to do. A need did not always constitute a call.

In my overflowing life, I am challenged to be still and listen for what should be on my list. Sometimes the good steals time and energy from the best. So I have tried to make it a habit to have a piece of paper handy as I start the day with my quiet time. At the top of the paper I usually write out the verse God gave me. Then, as things come to mind, I make my to do list. I pray over it and adjust it, if needed. Things not completed that day can always be carried over.

MRS. DEA IRBY

Father, help me to walk in the works You have placed on my to do list. Amen

Overcoming Temptation

> *There hath no temptation taken you but such as is common to man: but God is faithful, who will not suffer you to be tempted above that ye are able; but will with the temptation also make a way to escape, that ye may be able to bear it.* I Corinthians 10:13 KJV

There isn't anything we can do to keep from being tempted. Remember Satan tempted his Creator, Jesus. If he was brazen enough to try to cause Jesus to sin, you can be sure he won't let you get away without being tempted. All around us are temptations. However, not all of us are tempted by the same things. The world tries to tell us that it is all right to tell lies, especially if it is to keep from hurting someone's feelings. That is one of my big temptations. I hate to have anyone mad at me or to think that I may have hurt someone's feelings. Some are tempted to seek affections outside the bounds of matrimony, especially when their husbands are working many hours leaving them alone. Some are tempted to find comfort in alcohol or drugs.

Although there are a wide range of temptations, there is not a single one that we will face that we cannot overcome as Christians. God graciously limits the temptations that the enemy throws at us and He always gives us a way of escape. Just because we have been given the ability to defeat temptation doesn't mean we can do so without a fight. Jesus is there to help us if we will let Him. If we allow Jesus to fill us, we won't cave in to the outside pressures of temptations.

Mrs. Bonnie Lambert

> *Please help me to be more like Jesus and overcome temptation, in Jesus' name. Amen*

For Such a Time as This

...And who knows but that you have come to royal position for such a time as this? Esther 4:14b NIV

It was a birthday present I would never forget that February 2003. My husband Jim received the news that his unit, Marine Air Group 39, was deploying the next day in support of Operation Iraqi Freedom. As a senior officer's wife, I needed to be supportive of my husband's position. Memories of Jim's gas mask lying on the couch next to his flight helmet with "Chaps" in red letters still linger. How could I be at peace and place Jim in the Father's hands during this time? In March the war broke out and Jim's unit received the first casualties. God directed my steps to be at the family meeting to address the loss of our Marines with the young enlisted and junior officer wives. There were many tears, hugs, and words of comfort that I was able to express to these hurting ladies. We listened as the Commanding Officer gave the report. Many women asked if my husband, the chaplain, could check on their husband or boyfriend. I was able to send word to Jim. This began a special time of Jim and I partnering in this ministry for the Lord.

The next few weeks, God gave me the strength and ability to help with memorial services. I assisted with two Casualty Assistance Calls, where we notified wives of the death of their husband and supported and encouraged other officer wives. God's sweet peace definitely sustained me during those months. God had placed me at Camp Pendleton ("for such a time as this") and I know He gave me the strength to do His work at that time.

Mrs. Shirley J. Ellis

Lord, guard my heart and mind to serve you faithfully. Amen

Falling "In Love"

Love the Lord your God with all your heart... Luke 10:27 NIV

It is possible to fall head-over-heels in love with God. Is that a new concept for you? Remember, love is a relationship. God loves you. If you don't receive it and return the love, you won't be able to enjoy it. What generally happens when you fall in love? Think back to your first serious encounter. The young man who stole my heart was constantly on my mind. I wanted to spend every waking moment in his presence. I longed to talk to him and find out everything I could about him. I'm sure my feelings for him were no secret to those around me. It was evident in my behavior and in the big smile on my face. Should my love relationship with God elicit anything less?

As I grow in my intimacy with our Lord, I find myself wanting to spend more time in his presence. I long to find out more about him, and I use every source available to accomplish that. I want to do the things that please him. Not only do I enjoy talking to him, I love to talk about him, telling others how great he really is! Some people have problems with understanding such an intimate relationship with God. Yet, throughout the Bible the imagery exits. In the Old Testament, Israel is referred to as the Bride of the Lord (Isaiah 54:5). In the New Testament, Christ's deep love and commitment to the body of believers is compared to the marriage covenant (Ephesians 5:22-32). So go ahead, enjoy the greatest love relationship possible!

MRS. HELEN KRUDOP

Precious God, help me not only to be a ready recipient of your amazing and constant love, but faithful to return it to You. Amen

Just Give Me Jesus

Be still, and know that I am God; Psalm 46:10a NIV

One of my favorite African folksongs goes like this: "I heard my mother say, I heard my mother say, I heard my mother say, Give me Jesus, give me Jesus. You may have all this world, give me Jesus. Oh, when I come to die, give me Jesus. You may have all this world, give me Jesus." The reason I love this song so much is because it sums up life for me. I can be so busy with all the things of this world but when the rubber meets the road, it all boils down to what I have done with Jesus.

I heard the story of a little girl who went with her mother to an Easter play where as part of the production the crowds were yelling for Barabbas to be released instead of Jesus. The little girl got very upset, stood up in her seat, and began to yell, "Give me Jesus. Give me Jesus." This little girl realized the most important person in the world is Jesus and she wanted Him. So often I find myself in a hurry to spend time with Jesus, but most of the time it is on my own terms. I pray, I read God's Word, and I leave my quiet time without even giving Jesus any time to speak to me. Today's Scripture portion tells me that the only way that I will get to know God is to be still in His presence and listen to His quiet voice in my heart. When I do this, Jesus will become my closet friend.

MRS. JANICE UPTON

Dear Jesus, please help me to be still and know that you are God. Amen

For Powerful Results, Apply Here

But you will receive power when the Holy Spirit has come upon you. . . Acts 1:8a NASB

My daughter and her family served on the mission field in Brazil for nine years, and I was often the beneficiary of their cultural experience. I have created some delicious new dishes after experiencing their tasty food. The metropolitan area of Brazil where they served also had some enviable (and quite affordable) pampering customs: full body massages, manicures, and pedicures, which I got to experience. I was given a wonderful hand and foot lotion that helps dry skin. I would apply a bit of that lotion on my hands and rub them all over. It felt moist as I began to spread the lotion, but as I continued wringing my hands, it soon began to slough off dry skin. After washing my hands, I applied a moisturizing lotion. Oh, that felt supreme! I didn't realize how rough my hands were until they weren't any more!

I pondered this process. If I had not applied the lotion but had vigorously rubbed my hands together, wringing them with diligence, I would not have achieved the same result. It would have been futile. No matter how sincere I was, the results would not be the same as they were using the lotion. Then I likened this process to the work of the Holy Spirit. How often in my Christian walk have I tried to diligently work off the dead skin of sin or sinful habits in my life!Without applying the "lotion" of the Holy Spirit, I am powerless. Oh, maybe I will feel better because I worked hard at change, but it is still futile. Just remember, for powerful results, you have to make the application.

Mrs. Dea Irby

Father, help me not to act in my own strength but to submit to the work of the Holy Spirit. Amen

Are You Serving Without Sitting?

But only one thing is necessary... Luke 10:42a NASB

Have you ever said, "If I don't do it, who will?" Are you so busy taking care of everyone and everything that you don't take care of the most important thing? What is the most important thing in your life? Is it your family or your job? Maybe it is a responsibility in your church. Are you consumed with health and fitness? All of these are good things, but are they the best thing? Of course not! Most Christian women know they need to sit at the feet of Jesus and be filled. Our problem is we know it, but we don't do it. We need to remember that we must sit before we can serve.

We often hear, "Be still, and know that I am God." We must however, remember the rest of that verse. "I will be exalted among the nations, I will be exalted in the earth!" (Psalm 46:10 NKJV)We sit, not for ourselves, but for God. As we are filled with the fruits of righteousness, God is exalted. When we are filled with the love of Jesus Christ, our service brings glory to Him. How much time are you spending on all of your responsibilities? How much time are you spending with God? Which area needs more attention? Ask a trusted friend to hold you accountable to sit before you serve. Spend at least one more minute each day in prayer. Turn off the television and turn on songs of worship. God will be exalted!

MRS. KAREN A. DISHMAN

Holy Father, teach me to sit at your feet and be filled with your righteousness. You are exalted in all the earth! Amen

Every Naomi Needs a Ruth

...the Almighty has made my life very bitter. I went away full, but the LORD has brought me back empty... Ruth 1:20-21a NIV

During three decades of ministry, I've heard my husband sound like Naomi and I've felt that way myself. "I came to this church full of hope, but God has dashed all my dreams. My plans have backfired." When ministry becomes miserable, I go to Ruth. Like her, I can verbalize my commitment to my husband: "Where you go I will go, and where you stay I will stay" (1:16). We are a team until death, and we go through the bad stuff together with God's help.

Notice that Ruth asked Naomi's permission before taking action (2:2). When I discern "the answer" and dump it on my husband, he feels even needier. My avalanche of advice buries him deeper. Instead I should ask, "Do you think it would be a good idea to...?" "What would you advise another pastor with this problem?" Ruth helped another way by meeting Naomi's physical needs, in her case for food (2:14-18). I can do this for my discouraged husband as well. Does he need more rest? How can I make him feel important? Or pamper him? Do I need to un-clutter the house so he feels less overwhelmed? Most importantly, I can enjoy sexual intimacy with him. This lets us escape from cares, releases tension, and makes us feel good about ourselves. Ruth even agreed to Naomi's (probably crazy-sounding) plan: "I will do whatever you say" (3:5). If I support my husband's ideas—even wild ones—he begins to dream again. When my husband is negative like Naomi, I can be his reassuring Ruth.

MRS. MARCIA HORNOK

Lord, show me how to humbly minister to my minister-husband today. Amen

New Every Morning!

The steadfast love of the LORD never ceases; his mercies never come to an end; they are new every morning; great is your faithfulness. Lamentations 3:22-23 ESV

There is something to be said for those still and quiet moments in the morning before anyone else is awake. It's a time to be still before the Lord, to reflect on a new day to serve Him, to serve my family, and to serve the body of Christ. Watching the darkness fade with the new morning light, I am often reminded of how truly amazing our God is and how thankful I am that He is merciful and steadfast in His love.

It is much too common in my life to come to the end of a day thinking of the things I should have done differently (the shoulda, coulda, woulda scenario)—the way I handled something with my husband, children, or a friend. But it is encouraging to remember that the Lord is growing us in all these situations to be more like Him. We may have to admit we did something wrong, swallow our pride and ask for forgiveness, or delve into the scriptures to see how we should handle ourselves differently next time. But we know He still loves us and grants us mercy. And when we have done the hard thing of making our wrongs right, He grants us such peace in knowing that we have become a little more like Him. A peace like the still and quiet of a new morning.

Mrs. Vicki Woods

God, I praise You for showing such mercy to me. Thank you for your faithfulness and steadfast love. Amen

Supply-side Faith

But my God shall supply all your need according to his riches in glory by Christ Jesus. Philippians 4:19 KJV

My husband and I have always tried to live our lives in faith and to raise our children, from an early age, to do the same. But I have to admit that there were areas where my faith wasn't as strong as others. One of those areas was having enough money for gas for the car. My husband was working out of state and I was taking our three children every Sunday morning to Sunday School and church services. But I wasn't going back for Sunday evening services or Wednesday evening services because we didn't have enough money for gas. We lived in a small town in Oregon and our church was 25 miles away over dark mountain roads. Then one day my teenage daughter challenged my faith. One Sunday afternoon she asked, "Mom, aren't we allowing Satan to keep us out of church by not having enough faith for the gas?"

Yes, as you may have guessed, we went to church that night after stopping for one gallon of gas. I told the children that we were definitely going on faith as one gallon of gas was enough to get us there, but we wouldn't be able to get home again without the Lord's help. During the greeting time at the beginning of the worship service, someone placed some money into my hand. Through this individual, God supplied the gas for us to get home, but then, He always is our supply.

Mrs. Bonnie M. Lambert

Please help me to always have faith and trust You to supply all our needs, in Jesus name, Amen

Rachael Weeping for Her Children

Thus saith the LORD; Refrain thy voice from weeping, and thine eyes from tears: for thy work shall be rewarded, saith the LORD.
Jeremiah 31:16 KJV

Rachel, the mother of Joseph and Benjamin (Genesis 35:24) depicts those who mourned in the days of the prophet Jeremiah. Ramah, a town near Bethlehem where she is buried, is the place her descendants would assemble to be carried away into captivity. (Jeremiah 40:1). Rachel refused to be comforted and her cries have been heard throughout many generations. Her sorrow is expressed again in Matthew 2:16-18 as she weeps bitterly for the lives of her Bethlehem children who were taken tragically during the reign of Herod. Despite Rachel's tears, Jeremiah presents a message of hope: A return of His people and a promise of blessing for the future.

Food For Thought: 1) Rachel pleaded with God for children (Genesis 30:1), had two sons, and died in sorrow (Genesis 35:18-19); 2) Rachel is encouraged to stop weeping. Her work in child rearing is promised to be rewarded (Proverbs 22:6); 3) In what ways is the calamity in Bethlehem part of the same picture that began in Jeremiah 31?; 4) Though Israel's immediate situation looked grim, God's compassion never fails. Ultimately, God has offered salvation through His Son to all who believe (Luke 2:30-32); 5) How can we apply this Scripture to our lives, families, and church? Jeremiah's message is bittersweet. Israel's present misery is in contrast to her future restoration.

Mrs. Lori Ciccanti

Heavenly Father, pour out our hearts like water before your face. Amen

A Life of Worship

Now unto him that is able to keep you from falling...
Jude 1:24 KJV

The business of ministry is overwhelming to say the least. There are times when you may find yourself in a dry place, feeling burned out. That can lead to feelings of despair and hopelessness. Those two things are in direct opposition to what God intends for His people. These feelings are especially dangerous to those in positions of leadership. How can one avoid such pitfalls? The answer is simple: live a life of worship. Jude 1:24 says, "Now unto Him who is able…" There is a bigger concept within these six words extracted from Jude's doxology, which will help us to live a life of worship. Here is the breakdown: "Now"—calls for immediate action. Stop whatever you are doing and focus intently on God. "Unto Him"—the next step is to reverence Him. Give God praise for who He is. "Who is able"—finally recognize that there is no impossibility in God. He is able to do exceedingly above what our mortal minds can conceive. Taking these steps everyday will bring about the desired results of living a life of worship.

Too many Christians believe that worship is something that we do on Sundays or at church only. This is a grave mistake that leads to spiritual dryness. Living a conscientious life of worship not only moves the heart of God but it keeps our hearts nestled in His. Remember, we cannot pass on something that we ourselves do not possess.

Mrs. B. Michelle Patillo

God touch the hearts of your people; give them the desire and ability to worship You in all that they do. Amen

The Joy of Brokenness

The LORD is near to those who have a broken heart...
Psalm 34:18 NKJV

One Bible person who knew what to do when broken-hearted was David. Many of his psalms originated from intense suffering. Becoming the king-elect brought more problems than privilege. If anointed while a teen, we can estimate that the period between knowing he would reign and actually becoming king at age thirty may have been fifteen or more years. During this time, he became King Saul's "Most Wanted Man." One of his lowest points came near the end of those years as a fugitive. After a successful skirmish, he and his men returned to their home base of Ziklag, only to find it raided. Their wives and children had been abducted and all their possessions stolen or burned. Then "David and the people that were with him lifted up their voice and wept, until they had no more power to weep" (1 Samuel 30:4).

Do you, like David, know that hopeless, option-less feeling? Just when you think things can't get any worse, they do. That's when David, in danger of being stoned by his own grief-stricken men, "encouraged himself in the Lord his God" (1 Samuel 30:6). How did he do that? The same ways we do. Broken-heartedness makes us submit to God, cast our cares on Him, and trust Him fully. It empties us of our selves so God can fill us with Himself. Elisabeth Elliot says, "It is He—not His gifts, not His power, not what He can do for us, but He Himself—who comes and makes Himself known to us. And this is the one pure joy for those who sorrow."

MRS. MARCIA HORNOK

Lord, I offer You my broken heart, knowing that your heart breaks with mine. Amen

Practicing Truth

My brethren, count it all joy when you fall into various trials, knowing that the testing of your faith produces patience. But let patience have its perfect work, that you may be perfect and complete, lacking nothing. James 1:2-4 NKJ

Lessons come in all forms, from the simple events of the day to the hard tests of life. Too often the desire to resist and resent the very things I pray for are present. The sermon on that particular Sunday was from James 1, "Count it all joy when you fall into various trials." As the day ended, I remember praying, Lord, help me to find joy in my trials. The next day, while I was placing some items on a shelf above the washer and dryer, the shelf fell and down came dozens of jars of pickles. You can imagine the mess…vinegar juice, pickles and spices behind the washer and dryer, under the washer and dryer and splattered into the hall floor. I wanted to curse, I wanted to fume, I wanted to walk away and see if it would magically clean itself up. Instead, the Lord gently reminded me of the sermon my husband had preached and my prayer of the night before.

Taking a deep breath I uttered a heart-less prayer of gratitude and began to clean. As the cleaning progressed the gratitude set in because… 1) I have pickle jars that weren't broken… 2) I had a washer and dryer… 3) There was a mop and cleaning supplies handy to help, and 4) I had the physical strength and stamina to clean. The list went on as my heart-less prayer became a heartfelt claim of God's provision. There have been many opportunities through the years to put into practice what began as a simple but profound truth. Some of those opportunities have been much harder and heart -wrenching than broken pickle jars, but all of them were gifts of learning and leaning on Him. Praise God for the many ways He shows truth.

Mrs. Carol Henschel

God, may the reality of your joy be the constant pursuit of our hearts. Amen

Day by Day

> *I affirm, brethren, by the boasting in you which I have in Christ Jesus our Lord, I die daily.* I Corinthians 15:31 NASB

A few years ago I was present at a youth gathering where the speaker asked all those who were willing to be martyrs to raise their hands. Without a minute's thought, hands went up all over the room. I glanced around the room looking at their bright faces and adventurous eyes. The exuberance of youth: their contagious excitement for the cause of Christ. It was difficult to get them off my mind even days later, as I reflected on what they had volunteered to do as quickly as they might volunteer to win a free CD. I wondered about how much thought they'd given to their decision since then. How would they prepare over the next few years if they were truly aware they might be called upon for the ultimate sacrifice. How does one prepare?

As Christians, should we be living as the early Christians did with the awareness that our very witness for Jesus could cost us our lives? In fact, true and deep Christianity that's more than skin-deep should cost us our lives—our daily lives. We are told to "die daily" to the world and to ourselves. I don't know about you but, for me, that's not an easy thing. All too quickly, I've told the Lord "I'll do anything for You!" only to struggle with keeping my mouth shut when someone hurts me or misunderstands me. Or maybe there's nursery duty at the church. Or maybe there's a children's class that needs a teacher. (Can't somebody else do it?) Dying daily is not only difficult, it's downright deadly.

MRS. JACKIE SHEPPARD

> *Help us to recognize and embrace that it's only as we die daily that we truly begin to live for You. Amen*

What If Only God Saw?

Beware of practicing your righteousness before other people in order to be seen by them... Matthew 6:1 ESV

How many things do we do so that others can see? Moms know how many things we do that nobody will ever see…change diapers (thousands of diapers), cut up the 100th hot dog, sing 10 verses of "Jesus Loves Me," wash chocolate pudding faces… we know the list is endless. So, what about at church? Pastor's wives know how many things are done that nobody will ever see. And yet, the things we may not want our church members to see—that's what they see. What about our relationship with Christ? Do we have a quiet time so that we can tell others about it? Do we memorize Scripture so that we can quote it perfectly in Sunday school? What if no one ever saw our walk with Christ? What if only God alone saw how much we loved Him? Would we be ashamed? Or would we feel honored to have such a secret with the Almighty.

Jesus said that when we pray we are to go into our closet; when we give, to do it in secret; when we fast, to put oil on our faces. Our relationship with Christ is not to be a secret. But what are our motives in our times alone with God…who are we doing it for? Would we still be as faithful if God were our only audience?

What if no one ever saw the works I've done,
the battles fought, victories won?
Would God's approval be enough for me, pleasing Him alone,
no one else to see?
If all were gone, no person to see
Alone for You may my works be.

Mrs. Melody A. Hertler

Father, help me to practice my righteousness for You alone. Amen

Mrs. Holy Spirit

I will make a helper suitable for him. Genesis 2:18b NIV

It all started in seminary. My husband's preaching teacher, Mrs. Bowden, had also been my college drama teacher. One of the dreaded elements of the senior sermon was to meet with her, watch a video of the sermon and listen to the critique of the delivery (not the content). I was invited to attend. The message was….well, I don't remember that part, but the critique was brutal. All during her evaluation she kept telling me, "Don't let him get away with that." My husband was definitely never out to impress anyone. He just preached the Word with passion and common language (and he still does, I might add). Well, as per her instructions, after each student "pulpit supply" sermon, I rolled out the list (literally) and gave him my assessment. I felt I was being his helper. Then I thought, why not expand my helping ministry to other areas of my husband's life? So I did.

It was much later in our marriage that God was able to reveal to me that I had been trying to be the Holy Spirit to my husband. He wasn't able to hear God sometimes because I was yelling so loudly. My ministry to my husband should be to pray for him and ask the real Holy Spirit to speak to him, to give him unconditional love and encouragement, and to be his number one fan. When I relinquished my role as Mrs. Holy Spirit, I realized that God was also able to work in me more. I still sometimes want to be Mrs. Holy Spirit but, praise God, He shows me the error of my ways before it's too late.

Mrs. Dea Irby

Father, forgive me when I am being Mrs. Holy Spirit. Amen

Called to Duty

Strength and honour are her clothing; and she shall rejoice in time to come. Proverbs 31:25 KJV

As pastors' wives, we realize that our husbands have been called to duty in the Lord's army. Not only called to duty but called to the front line. Just as military wives have to support their husbands while they are fighting in battle we, too, have to support our husbands on the battlefront. How can we be the strong support and prayer warriors that they need to help them fight the battle, while at the same time bringing honor to them and our Lord and Savior?

In the heat of battle it is easy to loose control and let our old natures take over. We want to jump in with both feet to defend our loved ones. I know that there have been times in my husband's ministry that I have wanted to. I have tried to keep my mind on the Lord. I found that if I waited for a minute and asked for the Lord's help before I opened my mouth, the Lord would speak for me. Or He would seem to put His hand over my mouth so that I wouldn't say anything at all. It was then that I was able to rejoice over the outcome knowing in my heart that whatever happened I had brought honor to my husband and to the Lord.

Mrs. Bonnie M. Lambert

Please clothe me with your strength and honor. Help me to be the helpmate You want me to be. Amen.

Free to Be Me

For we are God's workmanship, created in Christ Jesus to do good works, which God prepared in advance for us to do.
Ephesians 2:10 NIV

I became a pastor's wife at 19 years of age. I grew up knowing I would be anything but that…you know how God takes you places you never expect to be and lets you experience things as only He can. I was in my mid-twenties and we were serving a church of sweet people. Their previous pastor's wife, from all accounts, was perfect. Her children never misbehaved, her house was always perfect, and she was a great cook. I felt that I could never measure up. On a particular day a wise and sweet saint from the church came to visit. I kept apologizing for all the things that were out of place and out of order. She saw my frustration, but she saw more than that. She sat me down and said, "Carol, you are not our previous pastor's wife. She is a treasure, but so are you. Your strengths are different and your giftings are unique. Rest and be yourself, you'll find our church just wants to know you!"

Those simple words changed my perspective and allowed me the freedom to fail (and succeed) and pursue a relationship with this congregation without worrying about comparison. Thank you, God, for that freedom.

Mrs. Carol Henschel

Lord, Thank you for making me…ME! I ask that you continue to teach me the great freedom of being what You made me to be, nothing more and nothing less. Amen

Life-itosis

Their robes were not scorched, and there was no smell of fire on them. Daniel 3:27c NIV

Halitosis is a condition commonly referred to as bad breath. Years ago a television commercial was created that warned about "house-itosis" and offered cures. It set me to thinking about smells in the Bible. A soothing aroma is mentioned in the sacrificial instructions over and over: "But you shall present a burnt offering, an offering by fire, as a soothing aroma to the LORD" Num. 29:6 (NASB). The Bible also tells us that our prayers are a sweet aroma to God. Another instance of a not so pleasant smell is in John 11:39, "Jesus said, 'Remove the stone.' Martha, the sister of the deceased, said to Him, 'Lord, by this time there will be a stench, for he has been dead four days'" (NASB).

As I thought about all these instances, the story in Daniel came to mind. Three men were thrown into a fiery furnace. But they were joined by a fourth man. The men who threw them into the fire were burned up because the fire was so hot. Yet the three children of Israel were able to come out alive and well and "smelling like a rose," so to speak. Christians are instructed to be in the world, but not of the world. Isn't this what happened to these men? Christ joined them in the fire and they escaped without being burned or even smelling like smoke. As we live in the world, being salt and light, our lives should be a sweet aroma to God and to others. The only way this is possible is to walk with "the Fourth Man." The next time you brush your teeth and gargle with mouthwash to make sure you don't have halitosis, check your spiritual aroma to make sure you don't have Christian life-itosis.

MRS. DEA IRBY

Lord, make my life a sweet aroma in your nostrils. Amen

Hurry, Lord, I'm Waiting!

Wait on the LORD; be of good courage, and He shall strengthen your heart; wait, I say, on the LORD! Psalm 27:14 NKJV

Waiting has never been one of my strong points. When I was a little girl my father was a traveling salesman for a farm implement company, and I would often go on the road with him. I looked forward to the rare showrooms that had miniature tractors I could pedal around while my father conducted business. Otherwise, I was supposed to sit quietly and wait. Without the miniature tractor to entertain me, I was soon stomping around looking as bored and sullen as I could so my father would hurry the order with his client. Sometimes I would tug at his jacket and interrupt his conversation with, "When are we going to leave, Dad?" and "How much longer?" My father was conducting business for the sake of our family. He had our interests at heart; he was trying to make a living to provide for us. But I was bored and thinking only about myself. I wanted him to hurry because I didn't want to wait. I wanted what I wanted, and I wanted it now.

I wonder how many times we act in the same impatient way with the Lord. We inwardly pout and stomp and say, "Hurry, Lord. I want an answer now. When is our church going to grow? When will my child turn back to you? When are you going to provide the finances I need?" Our Heavenly Father is telling us to wait while He conducts His business with our interests at heart. But we keep interrupting.

MRS. MARY ENGLUND MURPHY

Lord, help me keep my focus on You as I wait for You to work in my life. Amen

Words, Words, Words

Let the words of my mouth, and the meditation of my heart, be acceptable in thy sight, O Lord, my strength, and my redeemer.
Psalm 19:14 KJV

We use words cautiously at times, but at other times we speak too quickly or flippantly. We can use words lovingly when that emotion is felt. We speak at times even when we are not certain of the right thing to say. Words are important. Through words we offer our ideas to people as seeds or bullets. Sometimes words are unkind and become like bullets that hurt feelings or kill relationships. But words used as seeds can take root and become like flowers beautifying everything around them. We live in a noisy world full of words and other distractions. Noise is so normal that silence can become a distraction. We may say, "It's *too* quiet around here." But I've found that I need silence at times. I need the words of people to stop, so that I can hear the words of God. I remember that when God spoke to Elijah, it was not in an earthquake, or wind, or fire, but in a still small voice. If our world is full of noise, how will we hear the still small voice of God?

One Sunday a little three year old was trying to tell his parents about the Sunday School lesson. He said that the first man and woman ate from the forbidden tree in the garden and God made them _________. He stopped because he could not think of the right word to finish the story. After several tries, he finally came up with words he thought were ok and said, And God made them "BAREFOOTED ALL OVER!" He carefully chose his words—and made himself understood. Let's be sure our words are also carefully chosen.

Mrs. Betsy McSwain

God, help us to be cautious about our spoken words to one another. Amen

Open Lines of Communication

...praying always with all prayer and supplication in the Spirit, being watchful to this end with all perseverance and supplication for all the saints Ephesians 6:18 NJKV

On March 19, 1972, news was made all over the world when Lieutenant Hiroo Onoda emerged from the Philippine jungle on the island of Lubang, nearly thirty years after he was deployed by the Japanese army to conduct guerrilla warfare during World War II. Due to severed lines of communication, he was never officially told the war had ended. For twenty-nine years, he ate coconuts and bananas while evading search parties he thought were enemy scouts. It would be an understatement to say that Lieutenant Onoda and his commanding officers had poor lines of communication.

I'm so glad that our prayer line of communication is never broken or jammed. Prayer is our two-way radio with God and how we partner with Him in warfare and in fellowship. It is so vital to life's battles that Jesus made it a priority in His earthly life and ministry. He knew the power of prayer and even instructed His disciples to pray for deliverance from Satan. Because prayer is our most devastating and powerful weapon in defeating the enemy, our lines of communication with our Commander-in-Chief, the Lord Jesus Christ, must remain open and secure at all times.

"What a friend we have in Jesus, all our sins and griefs to bear!
What a privilege to carry everything to God in prayer!
O what peace we often forfeit, O what needless pain we bear,
All because we do not carry, everything to God in prayer."
(Joseph Scriven)

MRS. MARY ENGLUND MURPHY

Heavenly Father, Forgive me for not exercising the privilege of prayer. May my lines of communication with you be always open. Amen

Facing Cancer

Do you not know that your body is a temple of the Holy Spirit, who is in you, whom you have received from God? You are not your own; you were bought at a price. Therefore honor God with your body. I Corinthians 6:19-20 NIV

The doctor said, "Shirley, you have the fastest and deadliest of all cancer, black melanoma. I will do immediate surgery. I will do everything I can to save your life, but I can't promise anything. With that, my husband Pete and I were left with the most challenging time of our lives. We had four small children, the youngest a one year old. The surgery lasted 6 ½ hours. The malignancy that started in a mole on the calf of my leg had spread to my groin. All my lymph glands had to be removed. For ten days it was feared my leg would have to be amputated.

Through the time of my illness, God blessed me with the joy of His presence and the comfort of His Word. The truth that I was God's property kept echoing throughout my soul. Many people were praying for me. It's amazing when you are going through a trial how good it is to hear the words, "I'll be praying for you." As people rallied to help us, we saw the body of Christ working in beautiful unity. All the gifts of the Spirit and also all the fruits of the Spirit were showered upon our family. As Bill Hybels says, "There is nothing like the church when the church does it right." Well, that was thirty-seven years ago. Today I know that each day is a gift and a privilege from the hand of a God whose ways are always good.

Mrs. Shirley Ann Unaru

Lord, help us to realize we are not our own. Help us to rest in your sovereign, good plan for our lives. Amen

The Secret of Contentment

I have learned to be content in whatever circumstances I am.
Philippians 4:11b NASB

Contentment! Does anyone else struggle with this eleven-letter word? My husband still has his favorite childhood book, "The Contented Little Pussy Cat." Why does my life not seem to parallel that fuzzy kitten, curled up, satisfied in his small little world? Media screams out to us, that life won't be quite right until we either possess, belong to, or become (fill in the blank).

One day I took a deeper look at Paul's call to contentment. Research revealed that my nemesis "contentment" means to "limit yourself in desires and actions." I realized that contentment was a purposeful choice, not an innate quality. Paul LEARNED the secret of contentment by taking the focus off his own needs, to more clearly see God's perspective. Back in the dictionary, I discovered that the three basic methods by which we learn are through study, instruction, and experience. Examining my life for evidences of learning, I reviewed recent unexpected events and trials. All of a sudden, the Lord crystallized my thoughts, helping me realize that these were meant for my greater good. If I were to take my eyes off myself . . . my expectations . . . and set my mind on things above, I could become more content with my life's ebb and flow. Combined with studying the richness of God's Word and receiving instruction from others, contentment was something I could potentially realize. But wait! There's more! Why did Paul include the word "secret," the only place in the Bible where it occurs? I believe that Jesus is that secret, giving us a gift that the world cannot give.

Mrs. Margie Campbell

Lord, help me to find my full contentment in You. Amen

My Father Knows Best

"For my thoughts are not your thoughts, neither are your ways my ways," declares the LORD. Isaiah 55:8 NIV

"Lord, are you there? Do you see what is going on in my life?" Have these questions ever darted through your mind? This past year these questions filtered through my mind. I didn't doubt God's wisdom or question His dealings in my life. I had complete confidence that He was doing what was best. I knew I didn't have to understand, I just needed to trust Him. In this year of extreme highs and lows, beginning with the births of two more grandchildren, the death of my father and the wedding of our two daughters, I have been on an emotional roller coaster.

God's grace is amazing, for in His faithfulness He directed me to the book of Jeremiah. As I was reading Jeremiah 24:1-7 and 29:11, I was overwhelmed by what the Spirit of God showed me from His Word. I am sure the Israelites felt deserted by God when they were taken as exiles to Babylon. They were uprooted from their homes, lands and everything familiar to them, yet it was God Himself who sent them away. But God promised, *"My eyes will watch over them for their good..."* God had not forgotten His chosen people. In His infinite wisdom, He had a far greater purpose for them. *"...I will build them up and not tear them down..."* He promised, *"For I know the plans I have for you"* declares the Lord, *"Plans to prosper you and not to harm you, plans to give you hope and a future"* (NIV). The same promises are true for us. The same God who watched over the children of Israel, is watching over us. How infinite His plans are for us!

Mrs. Patti Oliver

Father, You have brought me to this place in life for my good from your heart of love for me. Amen

A Family Ministry Team

Rejoice in the Lord always. Again I will say rejoice!
Philippians 4:4 NKJV

The opportunity to be a pastor's wife and the mother of a ministering team has been the source of abundant joy. For thirty-five years I stood alongside my husband as the helpmeet the Lord gave him in caring, sharing and loving the members of a precious church family. During those years, I felt that it was my calling to teach our children that they were a part of a pastor's family by design and not by default. My husband and I both emphasized to them the privileges and blessings enjoyed because we were a ministering team. Each Sunday they were urged to greet the older men and women in the church. They often shared these special experiences with us over dinner. It was important that we involved them wherever we could in ministry decisions.

One evening we promised to take the children Christmas shopping but my husband received a call from a man in the church. His newborn son was in Children's Hospital and was not expected to live. Rather than just tell our children that we couldn't go shopping, we shared this need. They all said, "Daddy, you have to go!" The next day it snowed and there was no school. We spent the whole day shopping with them. There is great rejoicing that comes from seeing your family share the same excitement about answers to prayer, the salvation of souls, and spiritual growth in lives. Today, three of our four children are in full time ministry and all are joyfully serving the Lord.

MRS. CAROL GREGORY

We rejoice, Lord, in the opportunity you gave our family to be a ministering team. Amen

Lessons in Simplicity

"Martha, Martha," the Lord answered, "you are worried and upset about many things, but only one thing is needed. Mary has chosen what is better, and it will not be taken away from her."
Luke 10:38-42 NIV

Do you ever feel like you are balancing too many balls in the air? The things we can control the least in life, matter to us the most. How can we determine what are our best priorities for this day, this life? Martha opened her home to Jesus and His travel-weary disciples. While she was busy preparing the meal, the pressure of the situation got to her. Especially as she saw her sister Mary (who should be in the kitchen, Martha thought) quietly and calmly at the feet of Jesus, listening to His every word. Martha was an "overdoer." She knew little of the word "simple." If she was going to do it, she was going to do it with extravagance. Her love affair with perpetual motion led her to stress and chaos. Like Martha, the busier we get the emptier we'll feel. Claire Cloninger wrote in *A Place Called Simplicity*, "Voluntary simplicity is choosing to live more frugally on the material side of life so we can live more abundantly on the spiritual side of life."

It seems the more we pack *into* our lives, the less we experience *of* our lives. We've become modern-day Marthas: busy, distracted, and empty. But what we need is to be like Mary: calm, focused, and fulfilled. Mary created pauses in her busy days to hear what the Savior had to say. She made time for the things that ultimately matter and for the One who eternally counts.

MRS. SHIRLEY ANN UNRAU

Lord Jesus, teach us to be more like Mary, knowing what is important and eternal. Amen

Living in the Light

I am the light of the world. He who follows Me shall not walk in darkness, but have the light of life. John 8:12 NKJ

Are you living in the dark? It might be a physical place; a country that does not worship the one true God or an inner-city apartment surrounded by poverty and addicts. Maybe it is an emotional state, such as depression or discouragement. There is darkness that comes from separation: death, divorce or distance from someone you love. Most people don't like dark places. Little children (and some adults) admit to being afraid of the dark. Many people sleep with a night light. (How can one little four-watt bulb make a child feel safe and secure?) Have you ever been in a completely dark room where you literally could not see your hand in front of your face? You turn on a night light and the darkness disappears. Darkness is merely the absence of light, so when light is present, darkness is gone. Darkness is driven away by the power of light.

I was in another country where there was spiritual darkness all around me. I could literally feel it. In the darkness however, I was not in the dark. I have never been more aware of the light within me than I was during my visits to temples and shrines in that country. You may think you are in the dark, but if you know Jesus you are not in the dark at all. You are in the light because His light shines within you!

Mrs. Karen A. Dishman

Dear Father, may I never fret over the darkness around me but show others the light that is within me. Amen

Size 9 ½ Snow Boots

*He who did not spare his own Son, but gave him up for us all—
how will he not also, along with him, graciously give us all things?*
Romans 8:32 NIV

I'm constantly astounded at how much in detail God answers prayer. As children, we learned that God doesn't always say "Yes." Sometimes He says "No" or "Wait." As adults, we accept that this is His sovereignty and also His way of showing us detail by detail what's good or purposeful for us.

One year we had a last-minute snow trip planned in April, when stores no longer stocked snow accessories. Our family didn't have snow clothing, so I borrowed from friends. I was able to collect snow boots and snow pants for everyone in the family, except for one pair of snow boots for one of my daughters. After exhausting my contacts and shopping with no success, I figured I'd put her in regular shoes and double up her socks. But I still prayed that God would answer my silly prayer request for size 9 ½ snow boots. Just days before our trip, I walked into a friend's house. She handed me a bag and asked, "Do you need size 9 1/2 snow boots?" I was speechless! How exact God is in answering prayer! He blesses us through details to show us how much He's paying attention to our needs. It is amazing how God loves us so much that He sent His only Son to die for us, and then He even answers our silly prayers.

Mrs. Daisy Wong

Lord, help me to not worry over details and things I don't have, knowing that You will supply all I need. Amen

How Can It Be?

Thou hast ravished my heart, my sister, my spouse; thou hast ravished my heart with one of thine eyes, with one chain of thy neck.
Song of Solomon 4:9 KJV

Insecurity plagues every feminine heart. Yet Christ comes with the warmest of reassurances in these words spoken lovingly to His Bride. We have ravished His heart! But how can this be? His own words answer our objections by defining our relationship. He calls us His sister, for we are related to Him by blood. He has made Himself our elder brother. What sweet relation! He calls us His spouse, for we are related to Him by choice. He has chosen us unto Himself and made us His bride. His own words describe the delight He takes in our service. His heart is ravished with just one glance from our eyes. Though we look through a glass darkly, and but peak at Him through the lattice, yet even our partial gaze of admiration is well pleasing to Him. He is ravished with one chain of our neck. Though this chain of service in His kingdom is encumbered by weakness and sin, yet our desire to please Him is His delight.

Lord, what comfort I find in your words! All that You delight in You have provided me. Our relationship is because of your blood and of your choice. It is your presence upon which I gaze; it is your kingdom in which I serve. You have fitted me to delight you, and in this I take delight! Forgive me for looking to my own unworthiness instead of your work. Your words give me courage. May I never hide from You, but rather may my heart's cry forever be… "Let my beloved come into his garden, and eat his pleasant fruits!"

Mrs. Jan Kimbro

Thank You, Lord. Amen

A Friend Who Cares

O magnify the LORD with me, and let us exalt his name together. I sought the LORD and he heard me, and delivered me from all my fears. Psalm 34:3-4 KJV

Have there just been times when you felt so blue and empty and lonely, as though there was no one who loved you, heard you or even cared that you existed? I think we've all been there one time or another. Or perhaps, you say that it's been many, many times. Or maybe you're there right now and are just wishing something...someone...somewhere would be there just for YOU!

Well, I've got Someone just like that who cares, loves you more than anyone in the world, and will be there any time or any place through thick and thin! That SOMEONE is my Jesus. He alone can give you the comfort and peace and joy that you need. There's a song that says, "Only Jesus can satisfy your soul--only He can cleanse your heart and make you whole." Believe me from personal experience only Jesus is absolutely true. He can be that wonderful Friend and Comfort that you're seeking right now. Remember, you're NEVER alone and there's ALWAYS hope as long as Jesus is alive. Do you know what? He still is and always will be. And because He lives, we all can face tomorrow.

MRS. GEORGIA M. SAWHOOK

Dear Lord, help me to remember that You're always there and that You'll never leave me. Thank you for your precious love. Amen

A Hebrew Mother's Faith

She named him Moses, saying, "I drew him out of the water."
Exodus 2:10b NIV

Jochebed, the name of Moses' mother means "Jehovah is her glory." Her name is only mentioned twice in Scripture, but it is a name that testifies to the strength of her character and faith in God. There is no doubt that Jochebed had a tremendous influence in the life of her son and family. Jochebed, against all odds, remained unintimidated by the threats of Pharaoh to harm her child. After hiding Moses for three months, Jochebed demonstrated great faith and courage in her sovereign God when she placed her baby in a woven basket-turned boat and placed him in the waters of the Nile River. As a result, Moses was found and adopted by Pharaoh's daughter. He received the best opportunities growing up in Pharaoh's court and being educated as a prince. This experience prepared him for the tremendous task God planned for his future. Moses went on to become one of the greatest leaders of Old Testament history. Jochebed serves forever as a testimony to the importance of trusting in God and putting faith in action.

FOOD FOR THOUGHT

1. How did God reward Jochebed's faith? And what irony do you see in this story?
2. Note: Moses' parents are recorded in the great chapter of faith—Hebrews 11.
3. In what way does God use the waters of the Nile River to picture salvation?

Jochebed's faith was timely rewarded as God fulfilled the great purpose He had for her son.

Mrs. Lori Ciccanti

"Restore us, O LORD God Almighty; make your face shine upon us, that we may be saved" (Psalm 80:19). Amen

My Heap or His pillar?

And the LORD went before them by day in a pillar of a cloud to lead them along the way, and by night in a pillar of fire to give them light... Exodus 13:21a ESV

I love the fast paced, fulfilling days of my life. But sometimes I struggle with how to fit all the pieces into those 24-hour days God created. My mind whirs with what needs to be studied, cooked or cleaned before that next activity; who needs a call, a note, a text or an e-mail before 5 PM.? My sermon notes usually have to-do lists in the margins. I really love the hustle and bustle of my life, until I fall exhausted in a heap. Weeping in that heap, I'll cry out, "God, where are you in this mess? How did I get here AGAIN?"

In answer the Lord often brings a children's song into my mind. "One step at a time, Only one step at a time, This is the way the Lord will lead you, One step at a time. Take that one step carefully, Walk that one step prayerfully; This is the way to victory, One step at a time" (CEF Press).

The words of the little song remind me of how God led His children in the wilderness. And I ask myself: Do I want my heap or His pillar? The walk of faith is not one of racing ahead like a kid on her new bike nor dragging along like a toddler on a walk. Instead, it is walking one step at a time with the eyes of my heart focused on Him.

Mrs. Lori Cherland McCune

Lord, help me remember how perfect your timing and your "to-do lists" are and show me how to order each day according to Your plan. Amen

God's Inscrutability

For who has known the mind of the LORD? Or who has become His counselor?
Romans 11:34 NKJV

For the first anniversary of 9/11, I organized an evangelistic outreach for our church. We rented a park pavilion and advertised a free breakfast, inviting all the fire fighters and police officers in our area. We prepared for 75 visitors. That morning it rained for the first time in two months, and the temperature set a record low for that day of 53 degrees. No visitors came. The two fire fighters who did attend got called to a fire right after the flag ceremony. I know of a minister's wife who finally conceived a baby after nine years of infertility. One week before the due date, the baby strangled in her cord and died. Sometimes we simply can't understand what God is doing or why. He is inscrutable to us. Inscrutability means that God does not have to explain Himself. If I could interpret Him or figure Him out, I would be His equal—how ludicrous (and prideful) is that? Often He does reveal possible reasons for our trials, but that should not be my focus. It took a period of mental illness to teach King Nebuchadnezzar that no one can say to God, "What have You done?" (Daniel 4:34-35). Job learned it after losing everything dear except his critical wife (Job 40:1-5). God answered Job's questions with interrogation not explanation, teaching us that God does not have to defend Himself. Even if my adverse circumstances seem inexplicable and senseless, I can trust God anyhow. He knows what He's doing in my life, and that means I don't have to.

MRS. MARCIA HORNOK

O Lord, You are all-wise, all-loving, and all-good—and that's all I need to know. Amen

The Bristly Bush Posture

But he himself went a day's journey into the wilderness, and came and sat down under a juniper tree; and he requested for himself that he might die, and said, "It is enough; now, O LORD, take my life. I Kings 19:4 NASB

Have you ever found yourself in the place of utter loneliness, ready to give up? Elijah has just come off the incredible victory at Mt. Carmel, but now Jezebel is out for his head. He flees from northern Israel to a southernmost city where he leaves his servant and goes farther into the desert. He then throws himself under a bristly bush (juniper trees are not the majestic tree we would like to imagine). He prays to die.

What is God's response to this depressed prophet? He sends the Angel of the Lord to minister to him. He then sends him back to the beginning—to Mt. Sinai where it all began—the place where God first revealed himself to Moses and established His covenantal promises. Here God reveals himself to Elijah in a gentle, blowing breeze—a still, small voice. He reassures Elijah that he is not alone. Often verse 18 is interpreted in a judgmental tone for Elijah to "pull himself together" but the context is all about God's promises and gentleness. This reequips Elijah for ministry. And by the way, Elijah never does die! When we are completely at our end God gives the greatest gift of all: Himself. He reminds us that we are not alone. Not only do we have Him, but He also surrounds us with His children. Be reassured by His gentle promises.

Miss Leah Hornok

Father, remind me of your gentle presence, reassure me with your promises, and reequip me to do your ministry. Amen

Rolling, Rolling, Rolling

Uphold my steps in Your paths, that my footsteps may not slip.
Psalm 17:5 NKJ

My two-year-old daughter found her sister's rollerblades and for about a half hour, she tried on her own to put them on. When she finally succeeded, she tried to stand up and roll. She tried and tried, but one foot would go one way and the other foot would go the opposite way. This must have gone on for another half hour! Then I brought her to the couch and taught her to hold on. She discovered that by holding onto the couch, she could not only stand up, she could roll!

That cute little incident reminded me how I often try to stand on my own, only to discover that my steps are wobbly and uncertain. I think I know what to do or where to go next, so I don't consult with the Lord or wait for His answer. We might be able to stand on our own for a time, and we might even enjoy a smooth ride for a while, but without God upholding us, we will surely fall. Have you rolled away from the Lord only to rely on yourself? Come back to Him and allow Him to uphold your steps, so that your footsteps will not slip.

Mrs. Daisy Wong

Lord, help me not to run ahead of You but to rely on You to hold me up so that my footsteps will not slip. Amen

What Thorns Teach

It is good for me that I have been afflicted, that I may learn Your statutes. Psalm 119:71 NKJ

While our home was being repaired after a fire, we lived in a rented house for a year. One Saturday my doctor called with results of my recent biopsy—a rare form of cancer. As I hung up the phone, the doorbell rang. There stood my prayer partner, Phyllis. (God directs the play of our lives and everyone comes in on cue!) Before I told her about the doctor's report, she asked me a pointed question. "What have you learned about God because of your fire?" I had no answer. My focus had been on what we had lost, all the inconveniences, problems with the insurance, decision overload.... What had I learned about God?

My new perspective started me on a quest. I studied 2 Corinthians 12:7-10 and found at least three benefits from thorns in our flesh: 1) It eliminates pride (mentioned twice in verse 7). 2) It enables me to learn the sufficiency of God's grace (v. 9). 3) It exchanges my weakness for His strength (v. 10). Perhaps another, less direct one comes from verse 8--it escalates my prayer life. In other words, chronic "thorns" that irritate me can be useful for short-circuiting my pride, showcasing God's grace, super-charging me with Christ's power, and strengthening my communion with God. Eventually I saw God's goodness--in spite of a house fire and cancer surgeries. In my journal, I recorded twenty-six blessings we would have missed without those trials. Even though God's sanctification process hurts, my thorny circumstances can produce God-intended benefits and blessings.

Mrs. Marcia Hornok

Help me keep my focus on You, my Lord, not on my losses. Amen

God Makes No Mistakes...

And we know that all things work together... Romans 8:28 KJV

Have you ever wondered if God made a mistake? I must admit to those thoughts as I faced eleven hours of surgery for bilateral mastectomies and reconstruction. You see, I explained to God, that I had watched my mother die from breast cancer the year before. I was a pastor's wife who had surrendered my life to Him. I had three young children who needed their mother. My husband and I were ministering in a growing church. Surely God made a mistake. Six years later, while in Ukraine on a mission trip, God reminded me that He does not make mistakes. I stood in a hospital ward with a woman who had recently had breast cancer surgery. I watched in horror as an IV pole, supposedly containing chemotherapy, was rolled from one woman's arm to the next. I was drawn to the bed of a woman whose cancerous lymph nodes had been removed that morning. A dirty linen cloth had been folded and placed under her arm in lieu of sutures. I shared with this woman, obviously frightened and in pain, that I understood her fear. I showed her the scars under my own arms and explained that I had undergone the same surgery. Because I could relate to her difficulty, she allowed me to tell her about my Jesus. Bed by bed, I moved around that room and led the women to a glorious faith in Jesus. They listened intently to me simply because I had walked where they were walking.

As I left the hospital in Ukraine that day, God reminded me that He makes no mistakes.

MRS. DEBBIE BRUNSON

Jesus, please use my life to point others to You. Amen

Learning from the Pain

Dear friends, do not be surprised at the painful trial you are suffering, as though something strange were happening to you. But rejoice...that you may be overjoyed when [God's] glory is revealed.
I Peter 4:12-13 NIV

Several years ago, one of my grandsons was helping me bake Christmas cookies. We had just taken a freshly baked batch from the oven when a visitor came to the door. While I was otherwise occupied, my grandson leaned over the cookies to get a good whiff of their fragrance. In the process, he laid his arms across the hot cookie sheet, which left noticeable burns on both arms. Being a high-functioning autistic child, he has a very high tolerance for pain. He was not aware of the pain, so he didn't realize the potential danger of the situation. Pain might seem like a bad thing to us, but pain has its place in the order of things. If we can't feel pain, we might be in harm's way and not realize it. The Scripture passage above offers us good insight regarding the things that cause pain in our lives and how it *can* be helpful. Rather than perceiving the pain as detrimental or unbearable, we can actually use the painful experiences in our lives to help us achieve new heights in our relationship with God.

God uses the soaring eagle as another unique example of how we can weather the storms of life in Isaiah 40:31. When our painful experiences threaten to push us down, we are to let God lift us to new heights as we put our trust in Him.

Mrs. Helen Krodup

God, how graciously you use every aspect of our daily lives to draw us ever closer to you. Help us to listen to your voice as You teach us. Amen

The World at Our Door

For I was hungry and you gave Me food, I was thirsty and you gave Me drink. I was a stranger and you took Me in.

Matthew 25:35 NKJ

A few years ago, the Lord led us to leave a wonderful church where my husband was pastoring in a southern town and move to Atlanta to pastor a church in the heart of a vastly changing culture of Asian, Indian, African, Middle Eastern and Hispanic immigrants. In short, it was a world at our door. What a change from our sedate setting where life was predictable and everyone spoke "Southern English." We found that we could choose to wall up, isolate ourselves and keep everything as close to normal as possible. Or we could engage the culture around us. We couldn't deny the changes happening daily as more and more immigrants moved into the homes and shopping areas near the church, and we couldn't live with ourselves if we ignored it.

Soon, God began adding multiple language congregations into our fellowship. Every Sunday looks like a mission conference as people flood into every space available for worship in their heart language. It's truly like being missionaries to the world right here in America, right at our door. More and more, our members are learning to reach out to the world, both here and abroad. I won't say it hasn't been inconvenient at times. But, it has been worth it, so wonderfully worth it! As a church, we are extending the arms of the Lord toward the community where we are. And we're getting a glimpse of what heaven will look like when every tongue and tribe bow before Him!

Mrs. Robin Hall

Lord, open our eyes to the world around us--the world at our very own doorstep. Amen

The Craving for Spiritual Food

Like newborn babies, crave pure spiritual milk, so that by it you may grow up in your salvation. I Peter 2:2 NIV

Growing up in a Christian home gave me the privilege and opportunity to observe first-hand a young believer "craving spiritual milk." My mother was a young Christian in my early years. I remember watching her devouring God's Word and praying. Even when I didn't see her reading and praying, I knew she faithfully found time to spend with the Lord and learn from His Word. When I was young, I didn't appreciate her godliness, but as an adult I realize just how blessed I was for that heritage. Peter told his readers in 1 Peter 2:2, "Like newborn babies, crave pure spiritual milk, so that by it you may grow up in your salvation."

This imperative given by Peter for first century Christians holds true for us today. We are to long for and be eager for the nourishment that we can receive from reading God's Word daily, just as a newborn baby longs for milk. It is so easy to get caught up in the busyness of our days that we neglect the time we should spend in the Word and in prayer. I would venture to say that the majority of Christians struggle in this area. There is a continual tug of war pushing and pulling in the lives of believers for their time, for their focus and for their energy. Peter encouraged believers in 2 Peter 3:18 to, "Grow in the grace and knowledge of our Lord and Savior Jesus Christ..." That is an imperative for us to "be continually growing." Our spiritual growth is a process that takes time. Are you eager to devour God's Word? Is there a craving in your spirit for spiritual milk? Are you growing spiritually?

Mrs. Patti Toliver

Dear Lord, I pray that I will be like the deer that pants for streams of water, with a hunger and thirst that can only be satisfied by having a deepening relationship with You. Amen

Sufficient Grace

> *"My grace is sufficient for you, for My strength is made perfect in weakness." Therefore most gladly I will rather boast in my infirmities, that the power of Christ may rest upon me. Therefore I take pleasure in infirmities, in reproaches, in needs, in persecutions, in distresses, for Christ's sake. For when I am weak, then I am strong.*
>
> II Corinthians 12:9, 10 NKJ

God is fully aware of our struggles and weaknesses, but rather than condemn us, He wants to show his strength through us. I have more weaknesses than I would like to admit and sometimes I want to give up. But the Lord wants to take those weaknesses and turn them into strengths. For every failing in me, I find victorious strength in Him. When I'm fearful of failure, He gives courage (Joshua 1:9).When I waver, he gives perseverance (2 Peter 1:6). When I'm confused, He gives wisdom and direction (Proverbs 3:5-7).When I feel guilty, He is merciful and forgiving (Psalm 145:8-9). When I'm proud, He shows me how to be humble (I Peter 5:5b-6).

When I doubt, I find faithfulness in Him (I Peter 4:19). When I'm anxious, He teaches me patience (James 1:2-3).When I'm lazy, He teaches me diligence (Proverbs 12:27). When I'm sad, He fills me with joy (Nehemiah 8:10b).When I allow myself to be deceived by the lies of the enemy, He is truth and all that is honest (John 14:6). When I'm dissatisfied with myself, He makes me content in himself (Philippians 4:11). When I feel conflict, He gives peace (Philippians 4:7). And when I'm defeated, he gives victory (I Corinthians 15:57-58).

MRS. MARY ENGLUND MURPHY

Father, thank you that your grace is working your strength through someone weak like me. Amen

On Call

I will say of the Lord, He is my refuge and my fortress: my God; in him will I trust. *Psalm 91:2 KJV*

There is hope and assurance of God's guidance as we walk daily. One Saturday my husband and I were going into Wal-Mart and saw several chartered buses stopping. Military men and women were going into the store also. We spoke to several of them and asked where they were from and where they were going. They told us they were from a military base in North Carolina and were headed to Norfolk, Virginia, to be deployed on Sunday morning. We wished them well and told them that we would be remembering them.

As I thought about the thousands who are deployed for our country's safety and freedom, I also thought about how we must be thankful and prayerful for them and our leaders. We have an awesome task--to be on call as the Marines, Navy, Army, Air Force, and Reserve have been in the last few years. As Christians we, too, are on call daily. Be in touch with the One who is in control—God. We pray for peace and safety for our military and for our country.

MRS. BETSY MCSWAIN

Bless us dear Lord, and help us to be on call for You in our world of need. Amen

Two are better than one, fecause they have a good reward for their labor. For if they fall, one will lift up his companion. But woe to him who is alone when he falls, for he has no one to help him up.
Ecclesiastes 4:9-10 NKJV

Although born of noble birth, the Marquis de Lafayette left France and his family to travel thousands of miles to pledge support to a man he didn't know and to a cause that wasn't his own. He joined the Continental Army as a volunteer. In fact, he believed so passionately in the cause that he pledged his personal fortune. It wasn't his country or his battle, yet he fought willingly, bravely, and humbly under the command of General George Washington. At only nineteen years of age, he was given the rank of major general. Notwithstanding Lafayette's leadership qualities, perhaps his most vital role was one of support to Washington. He promoted Washington's interests, gave wise advice, and offered a listening ear and encouraging words. When other officers proved disloyal and tried to have Washington relieved of duty, Lafayette warned him and steadfastly defended him. Together these men planned military strategies, fought side by side, suffered hunger and exposure, agonized over defeats, and celebrated victories. Though more than twenty years separated them in age, their friendship lasted until Washington's death.

We all need a Lafayette in our lives: someone who understands what we are fighting for, has faith in our cause, and will stand by in times of need. We need someone who will be honest, loyal, understanding, and encouraging—someone who will fight alongside us, even if it isn't his or her battle.

MRS. MARY ENGLUND MURPHY

Father, Help me to stand in loyalty with my brothers and sisters in Christ. Amen

Outside My Kitchen Window

Are ye not much better than they? Matthew 6:26 KJV

I love to do the dishes at my house. It's a mindless task that affords me the opportunity to be still of heart. Often, after my chore is completed, I find myself lingering as a captivated spectator. You see, I've been blessed with a large picture window above my kitchen sink. It's a single pane of glass, and when it is very clean I can hardly tell that I'm not standing in my back yard. Outside this treasured window is a window box, which I fill in the spring with cascading purple and pink petunias. In front of my window is an ornate iron table, and in the center of this table sits a pretty little bird feeder. This scene has been the stage for many quiet moments of meditation as I have stood and watched the birds sweetly feed. They act as if they feel so secure, confidently returning to the bird feeder over and over with no worry about depleting the supply. It's as if they know that the food is placed there on purpose just for them, and they trust the giver to have an endless provision. Once fed, they contentedly find a perch on which to rest and cheerfully sing their songs of appreciation.

What a sweet example of the confident faith and contented gratitude that my Father deserves from me. Somehow I'm challenged... "Behold the fowls of the air; for they sow not, neither do they reap, nor gather into barns; yet your heavenly Father feedeth them. Are ye not much better than they?"

Mrs. Jan Kimbro

Lord, help me to be even better than these birds in my back yard, confidently trusting your never-ending provision, and cheerfully singing your praises! Amen

The Mighty Shepherd

Behold, the Lord God will come with might, with His arm ruling for Him. Behold His reward is with Him, and His recompense is before Him. Like a shepherd He will tend His flock, in His arm He will gather the lambs, and carry them in His bosom; He will gently lead the nursing ewes. Isaiah 40:10-11 NASB

Isaiah 40 is one of my favorite passages in all of Scripture because it places the promises of God and the character of God side by side. Our Father never asks us to trust Him blindly; He gives reasons to trust Him. The chapter gives God's promise of redemption followed by characteristic after characteristic of Himself. Verses 10 and 11 particularly stand out because they are so opposite. Verse 10 speaks of God's power and strength as a mighty warrior, while verse 11 presents Him as a tender, compassionate shepherd. (The sheep described are the youngest, weakest ewe lambs, utterly dependent on their master for protection and provision.) These qualities of God are purposefully juxtaposed because they are two aspects that we naturally separate. In times of discouragement, we believe that God can help, but we question that He actually will help. We don't doubt God's power, but we doubt His compassion.

How many times have you prayed for the salvation of an unbelieving friend or family member, or the healing of a loved-one—hoping desperately for a miracle but secretly doubting that anything will actually happen? God promises that He is not only one-hundred percent willing but one-hundred percent able.

Miss Leah Hornok

Father, I pray trusting the sure foundation of your character, believing that You can and will do exceedingly, abundantly beyond what I can ask or even think. Amen

Where is God?

...I willl go to him, but he will not return to me.

II Samuel:12:23 NASB

"Your son will not live through the night." Those are words no parent wants to hear; yet those were the words spoken on December 9, 1991. Our newborn son had gone through open heart surgery one week earlier. After the surgery, the doctor walked into the waiting room and proclaimed the operation "text book perfect." The subsequent days, however, showed little improvement in our son's condition. Something else was wrong. Finally, the doctor pronounced the inevitable: "Your son will not live through the night." I held our precious son as he left this earth to be held in the arms of Jesus. Where was God? We knew God was all-powerful; yet He seemed inattentive to our cries. Why didn't He do something? We stood at a crossroads of faith.

That fateful night my husband and I wrestled with tragedy. In our wrestling, we came to several life conclusions. We did not know where God was, but we knew who God was. We did not know what God was doing, but we knew what God had done in the sending of His Son. He loved us enough to give His Son for us. Our relationship with God assured us of His presence in the midst of our pain. God had not abandoned us. He was walking with us. He felt our hurt, and He hurt for us. Even though we could not trace God's hand, we could trust God's heart. Our son never came home from the hospital, but our son has gone home to the Father. One day we will see him again. This is the promise of God.

MRS. KAREN A. DISHMAN

Heavenly Father, today I choose to trust your heart. Amen

JOY IN THE ASHES (Part I)

To grant those who mourn in Zion . . . the oil of gladness instead of mourning. Isaiah 61:3 NASB

Our phone began ringing just as I arrived home from grocery shopping. Noting it was my oldest brother Ron, I grabbed it quickly, despite the frozen foods in my car. After a quick greeting, he somberly said, "Dad and Mom's house burned down, and Dad died of smoke inhalation." Feeling like the blood had drained from my body, I tried to absorb the double ramifications of his statement. In shock, I handed the phone to my husband Bruce. As I sat next to him, my thoughts oddly went to an old movie scene. Superman had been busy saving the world when he realized that Lois Lane's car had fallen into the San Andreas fault, where she lay entombed. Taking history into his own hands, he flew around the world, reversing its rotation, turning back the hands of time to rescue her. I imagined myself attempting the same, opening up the backdoor for my elderly father, who died just a couple of steps from the oxygen he needed.

Realizing the impossibility of my thoughts, I numbly tried to absorb how this would impact our lives. Another thought jolted through me. Mom! But how is Mom? Where was she when the fire started? With the Pacific Ocean separating us, Hawaii seemed an eternity away from California. Mom had lost everything, including her husband of sixty years. How could I possibly prepare for seeing my dear mother and the ruins of our childhood home? With our flights arranged I would soon face this scene. I needed to run to my Heavenly Father for strength.
[to be continued in the next two devotionals]

MRS. MARGIE CAMPBELL

Help me to walk through the valley of the shadow of death. Amen

JOY IN THE ASHES (Part II)

You have taken account of my wanderings; put my tears in Your bottle. Are they not in Your book? Psalm 56:8 NASB

Our family had lived in our Southern California ranch house for 60 years. Besides being home to my parents and four siblings, it had been the gathering place for many extended family celebrations. Vegetable and grain fields surrounded us, along with fruit and nut trees, grapevines, flowers, and vegetable gardens in our expanded yard. All were tested by the intense heat of Imperial Valley's summers. The concept of square foot gardening escaped my Dad. Farmer John would purchase 400 gladiola bulbs at a time. And Mom was always willing to get her hands dirty. Known as "Sadie, the flower lady," her bouquets of flowers also adorned our church, and the retirement home nearby.

Our home was actually very old. Falling apart would be a fair description. But Dad was handy with duct tape and baling wire, and there was evidence around the house that his concept worked. "Why spend some of your inheritance?" was his standard reply to our desires to renovate. I guess Dad was right. It would have just gone up in smoke. Dad hadn't been feeling well. Farming had taken a continual toll on his body ever since a tractor accident ended his college career. He lived with pain. On our last visit, his coloring blended with the grey shirt he was wearing. His doctor discovered his anemia, and iron supplements were his "duct tape" cure. The question on all of our minds had been, "How will Mom take care of Dad?" God had a plan, but could we face His unique answer?
[conclusion in the next devotional]

MRS. MARGIE CAMPBELL

In times of distress, may I find comfort in your presence, Lord. Amen

JOY IN THE ASHES (Part III)

An excellent wife, who can find? For her worth is far above jewels. Strength and dignity are her clothing, and she smiles at the future. Her children rise up and bless her.

Proverbs 31:10, 25, 28 NASB

Bruce and I arrived two days after the devastating fire. My apprehension melted as Mom hugged me tightly, assuring me of her well-being. Okay, one hurdle. Mom was strong, at least for the moment, helping us deal with the grief. The next hurdle was driving out to our ranch. Would I crumble at the sight of the charred ruins, where my father had taken his last breath before stepping into eternity? Ashes and soot abounded as we stood before the blackened skeleton. My mother and two sisters joined us as we stepped up and over debris. I anticipated tears, but oddly, there was a quiet hush of peace. No one was crying. Precious memories came rushing in as the farmer's wife and daughters dug through the collapsed roof, discovering family treasures. We unearthed keepsakes, most unusable, except to help ease the pain. My mother's cross necklace and a quilt sewn by her mother were two cherished finds. There were even moments of laughter as the mischievous child in us walked across furniture that had been off limits.

Pages of our family Bible blew across the lawn, a testament to our Christian faith. I can only describe this event as a holy moment, enhanced by my mother's complete trust in Jesus. Three years later she continues in His grace, accepting His will. We children rise up to bless her. My father's autopsy revealed cancer that had eluded lab tests. In His great wisdom, our Heavenly Father took him home.

MRS. MARGIE CAMPBELL

Thank you, Lord, for evidences of your hand in times of loss. Amen

Focus on Joy

> *...Who for the joy set before Him endured the cross...Consider Him who endured such opposition from sinful men, so that you will not grow weary and lose heart.* Hebrews 12:2-3 NIV

God formed us in such a way that we cannot sustain ourselves emotionally without something to hope in—something good to anticipate. We who believe in Christ always have something to look forward to. Even if our prognosis is death, to die is gain because being absent from our bodies puts us immediately with the Lord (2 Corinthians 5:8). Nevertheless, it's all too easy to commiserate about our losses. It takes determination and spiritual power to meditate on the joys set before us.

I experienced this on a small scale recently. My daughter and her husband had moved to Scotland for graduate school in August 2005. We had not seen them in nearly two and one-half years. Then someone gave them airline tickets to come home for Christmas. We learned this around the same time I received a diagnosis of breast cancer. I decided that every time I stressed about the surgeries, waited for pathology reports, and read scary things on the Internet, I would force myself instead to focus on the joy of meeting Amber and Paul at the airport on Christmas Eve. It worked! The joy focus kept me from despairing over my present circumstances and feelings. God had provided for us to have Amber and Paul home for three weeks, and He would see me through the radiation treatments and a new lifestyle. My prognosis and future, with its sorrows and celebrations, are in His hands.

Mrs. Marcia Hornok

Thank You for the joy You have set before me, not only in your special blessings here on earth but also in my eternally secure future with You. Amen

So You're the Pastor's Wife...?

That they may teach the young women to be... Titus 2:4 KJV

We have all known godly older women that seem to fit the description that floods our minds when the term "pastor's wife" is mentioned: Spirit-filled, submissive, joyful. It is our dream to grow into a replica of this gray-haired saint that we all hold in high esteem. But surely this godliness takes years of Christian experience to develop. How can we fill the role of a pastor's wife when we ourselves are only at the starting gate? Titus 2 dissects for us the characteristics of that woman we all long to be. This description is of a wise woman, a loving and kind wife and mother--sound of mind and pure of heart—who happily builds her home while doing good to others, always with submission and obedience, glorifying God and His Word with every act.

Yet this passage does not describe the gray-haired saint we often dream about, but rather instructs those older women to teach the *younger* women what they can and should be! This is the description of a godly YOUNG woman! Spiritual power is not reserved only for the aged or experienced. Time and experience are not the source of spiritual power, Christ is the source and the joy that flows from His presence is our strength. Is God not able to grant power to even the young and inexperienced runner? Is it not His pleasure that we should be holy instruments, fit for the master's use while we are yet young?

MRS. JAN KIMBRO

Lord, use me and make me believe that you are powerful enough to glorify yourself through even me! Amen

My Goliath-Sized What?

For the eyes of the LORD move to and fro throughout the earth that He may strongly support those whose heart is completely His.
II Chronicles 16:9a NASB

I have often heard 1 Samuel 17 referred to under the preface of "Life's Goliath-sized Problems." However, I believe that it is more about a "David-sized heart." David is set in contrast to all other individuals in this story. Not only is he the antithesis to the unbelieving pagan, Goliath, but he is also contrasted to the soldiers of Israel. Instead of trusting God's power, all they can seem to think about is the materialistic reward that will go to the soldier who defeats Goliath. David also stands in contrast to his older brother, Eliab, who is filled with anger and jealousy instead of faith. Ultimately, David is contrasted with King Saul, a polarity that has been developing since chapter 14 when Saul began to rule. Saul was the people's choice, but David was God's choice. Saul is the tallest, strongest, most capable, but when the people need him most he is hiding in his tent! David seems to be the only one who sees the reality of God's power. This is why he is God's chosen weapon for victory. God could have defeated Goliath using anyone, but David was the only one whose heart completely belonged to God. This passage is less about overcoming life's giant-sized problems and more about having confidence in our giant-sized God.

Like David, learn to trust God fully, knowing that He has already won the battle. And be the kind of weapon that He can use.

Miss Leah Hornok

Father, help me to have a heart that is completely yours, so that you can use me for your purposes. Amen

You've Got Mail

For we are God's workmanship, created in Christ Jesus to do good works, which God prepared in advance for us to do.

Ephesians 2:10 NIV

Shortly after we moved to Kansas City, my family experienced some major losses. A week after our move my father died, and my husband discovered that the ministry opportunity he was planning on had fallen through. We had been at our former pastorate for 29 years. I now found myself trying to cope with grief, move into a new home, and begin a new teaching job in an environment of uncertainty and aloneness. Also for the first time in our marriage, my husband and I were without a church ministry and the ready-made extended Christian family that comes with it. What sustained me through those first difficult months was the continuous stream of cards and notes from our former church family. While mail at the end of the day provided comfort, each morning a long day still loomed before me as I drove to what was turning out to be a difficult teaching assignment.

One particular note from a friend, however, brought hope. Her encouragement ended with Ephesians 2:10 and the question, "What good works does God have prepared for you?" That became my prayer as I left the house each morning. "God, what good works would you have me do today?" The grief is still there but easing, the uncertainty of the future remains, and we are still searching for a church family, but there is a focus now for each day. There are good works God has for me to do. My job is to be open to them.

Mrs. Suzan Moyer

God, what good work would You have me do for You today? Amen

Regretfully

But as for me, you meant evil against me, but God meant it for good. Genesis 50:20a NKJ

Can one live long and get through life without regrets and if-only's? Probably not. Some things are beyond our control, while others we perceive as being entirely our fault. Perhaps when we get to heaven, we will learn that they did not do the harm we have always imagined. The regrettable incidences of our life might even accomplish God's purposes, as He weaves everything together for the good of conforming us to His Son (Romans 8:28-29). David regretted his sins involving Bathsheba, yet from their marriage came God's choice for the next king of Israel—Solomon, not any of David's previous sons. Peter regretted his triple denial of Christ, yet it insulated him from ever doing it again. Why did Jesus tell Peter he would die by crucifixion in John 21:18-19? How could that have encouraged him? It must have made Peter realize he would never again lie to protect himself from death. Since his future included dying as a martyr, that meant he would stay true to the end. Paul regretted his zeal in persecuting Christians before he himself became one, but he said, "This one thing I do, forgetting those things which are behind, and reaching forth unto those things which are before, I press toward the mark for the prize of the high calling of God in Christ Jesus" (Philippians 3:13-14).

Although regrets in this life are inevitable, they need not hold us hostage. We can trust God to comfort us in our present life and wipe away all tears in our future life with Him.

Mrs. Marcia Hornok

Lord, give me Joseph's perspective—that You accomplish your good purposes in everything I experience. Amen

Contentment as a Constant Pursuit

Keep your lives free from the love of money and be content with what you have, because God has said, "Never will I leave you; never will I forsake you." Hebrews 13:5 NIV

The older missionary was recounting her life in Africa and the faithfulness of God's people to send gifts while she and her family were serving this needy part of the world. Her voice shook with emotion as she recounted how God's people would send exactly what her children needed and often what they wanted… peanut butter, Pop Tarts, a Scrabble game, and the like. Her transparency was clearly evident as she told the group that her greatest struggle sometimes followed those special care packages. In those many prayed-for gifts and needed items, there was news as well as bits and pieces of a culture she had left behind. Her friends and home church sent magazines and catalogs that made this young missionary wife and mother struggle with discontent. She saw dishwashers, washing machines, carpeted floors, and clean glass doors. There was also jewelry, clothes and pretty frills that, if she could have them, would never have been appropriate in the red, dry dirt of her African home. Miss Vivian, the name we all called her, was in her late seventies as she shared of her bountiful life and her struggles.

As we sat in the pew listening to her, it brought us all face to face with our own discontent. We live among the dishwashers, washing machines, and all the other things she had missed, but the periodicals we picked up were making us just as discontent. We didn't need any thing. We just wanted the new stuff. We left our luncheon that day with a new awareness of the way discontent creeps in (or too often is invited in). Magazines and catalogs often feed our longings for the material and temporal while God waits for us to long for the spiritual and the eternal.

Mrs. Carol Henschel

Lord, help me to value what You value and to pursue contentment. Amen

Who's In Control?

For as the heavens are higher than the earth, so are my ways higher than your ways, and my thoughts than your thoughts.

Isaiah 55:9 KJV

At a routine appointment during my 31st week of pregnancy, my obstetrician sent me to Labor and Delivery and talked to me about the possibility of having the baby immediately. He wanted to deliver me to avoid possible liver damage and kidney failure brought on by my increasingly severe pre-eclampsia. In a quick blur, I was transferred to a facility with a Neonatal Intensive Care Unit, in case I had to deliver a preterm baby. At that moment, I realized I wouldn't be able to do all the things I planned to do before the baby arrived! In the midst of my thoughts and plans, I heard God's overpowering words, "...My ways [are] higher than your ways, and my thoughts than your thoughts." My panic and confusion were replaced by God's overwhelming peace. I came to the place where I accepted whatever plans He had for me and for my unborn baby. I learned how not to be in control of my life (if I ever thought I was). I learned to yield my plans to Him and trust His plans for my life.

Do you have plans that you didn't accomplish? Commit them to our Heavenly Father who knows us, loves us, and wants the best for us. That might also mean you have to let go of your plans and submit to His.

Mrs. Daisy Wong

Lord, help us to yield our plans to You and accept your plans for us, because your ways are higher than ours. Amen

Seeing the Truth

..."One thing I do know. I was blind but now I see!"
John 9:25 NIV

The disciples questioned Jesus about a man who was blind from birth. He explained that God allowed this to happen, not because of sin, but so God could be glorified. Jesus anointed the man's eyes and instructed him to wash in the pool of Siloam. The man obeyed the Master and received his sight. The blind man was a witness before the religious leaders explaining that Jesus was the source of his new sight. After being questioned the second time, the blind man reminded the religious leaders that he had already gone through the details of his healing, but they would not listen. Unlike his parents, the blind man refused to be intimidated by their authority. With confidence, he took a stand for the truth which completely eluded those who professed to be educated teachers of God's law.

FOOD FOR THOUGHT

1. Jesus states that He is "The Light of The World" and warns against spiritual darkness. How can self-trust and pride prevent us from seeing the wonders of Jesus?
2. This blind man's confession is one of the most powerful testimonies in the New Testament. His faith is developed in such a short time and blossomed in the face of criticism and even persecution.
3. The blind man's willingness to believe resulted from his earlier experience of Jesus' compassion and healing power. How can we follow Jesus' example in leading others into His Kingdom?

By receiving his sight, the blind man reveals the superficial attitudes of the religious leaders.

Mrs. Lori Ciccanti

Lord, may we ever be aware of the darkness that Satan would slip over our eyes. Amen

Recycling Comfort

So that we can comfort those in any trouble with the comfort we ourselves have received from God. II Corinthians 1:4b NIV

In 1998 our family experienced significant losses. At one point my husband called the head elder of our church and said, "I don't know what to do. I can't study, let alone preach. I can't do any ministry right now. What should I do?" Graciously, the church leaders told Ken to take as much time off as he needed, and our associate pastor handled all church functions. People ministered to us and our children in a variety of meaningful ways during the next several months. Gradually healing came, and we found our footing once again. Then our focus shifted back to ministry, and our desire to reach out to others returned. Being diagnosed with cancer that year taught me about the fragility of life and motivated me, more than ever before, to work for eternity.

What did I discover during that time when we could not help ourselves, let alone anyone else? That God does not waste our sufferings. Paradoxically, He can use our weaknesses more than our competencies! We may feel like we will never be useful again, but eventually God presents an opportunity and won't let us rest until we act on it. Soon we realize how much our investment in others compensates us for our own losses. Grief counselors say it takes time to reach full circle, but it happens when we begin moving beyond our own pain to comfort and help someone else. One of God's ironies is that the more we give away, the more we gain.

Mrs. Marcia Hornok

Father, help me to serve while suffering by passing on to others the comfort You have given me. Amen

The Path of Love

One of the scribes came and heard them arguing, and recognizing that He had answered them well, asked Him, "What commandment is the foremost of all?" Jesus answered, "The foremost is, 'HEAR, O ISRAEL! THE LORD OUR GOD IS ONE LORD;

Mark 12:28, 29 NASB

In the Chinese language, love is depicted by a cow letting a lion eat her tail so she can hide her little calf from his revenges. Historically, a mother's love is celebrated as the strongest of earthly love, followed by the love of a man and a woman who forge their way through good times and bad times to become one. A wonderful possibility and the glue that keeps the human world together. Without some form of love, our race would have been destroyed long ago. The first Christians were known by their love for one another. A new standard of love entered the world made possible by the truest Love that split the universe–Jesus, the Great Love-Man who came to die in order to teach us how to love and how to live. Following Him requires us to love.

Something within us rises up, putting ourselves in the way of Love. We want to be loved and we want to love, but how? Often we create strong cocoons of relationships that we call love, and maybe they are. In the deepest moments of our Christian experience, when we at last put our hearts before Him in spite of the structures we have created to substitute for Him, we hear Him speak to the Bride about loving as He loved. Can it be that He wants a Bride that loves like He did? Or, at least tries to love as He did. The Word is plain. He said there were two great commandments–Love God with all your heart and soul and love your neighbor as yourself.

Mrs. Jacquelyn Sheppard

Father, help us to LOVE with the LOVE of CHRIST. Amen

Love In Deed

Little children, let us not love with word or with tongue, but in deed and truth. I John 3:18 NASB

Could it be that He was really serious about our loving one another and loving the people of this world? We agree that it is by His name, His blood and His love that we enter Heaven, but what if we had to pass a different sort of test to enter Heaven? Say, for example, a test on how we lived our lives in reference to that Great Commandment. What if we were asked upon reaching heaven, *How well did you love one another?* Could it be that being "right" about doctrine and practices are not as critical to our Christian lives as being "right" about how we love? What would happen if our platitudes and attitudes toward love were stripped away and our actions were evident, as well as our words?

Can the world recognize Christians now by our love? I don't know about you, but I want to love like He commanded. And that means actually doing something about loving God and loving people. It means a new level of sacrifice in how I respond to AIDS in Africa and the homeless man in the most prosperous nation in the world. It means something about how I respond to my brothers and sisters in the faith when we don't agree. It means that my heart has to change, not theirs. If I know anything about Calvary's Love, my heart and life has to take on new and deeper revelations about love. And, frankly, it's time for us who call ourselves the Bride and the Body of Christ to change the way we are loving–not just the bruised and broken world of hurting people, but also how we love one another.

MRS. JACQUELYN SHEPPARD

Help us, Lord, to love not only with our words, but also with our deeds. Amen

Finding Strength in Gethsemane

For we do not have a High Priest who cannot sympathize with our weaknesses... Hebrews 4:15a NKJ

The Bible indicates Jesus experienced the gamut of human emotions and suffering. When He took His disciples to Gethsemane for the last time, He asked them to watch and pray with Him. But they slept. Even though He told them, "My soul is exceedingly sorrowful, even to death," (Matthew 26:38), they must not have taken Him seriously. Perhaps they rarely saw a "needy" Jesus. The concept that Messiah could delay His kingdom, or even die, may never have crossed their minds--although Jesus had predicted it. In Gethsemane Jesus, "offered up prayers and supplications, with vehement cries and tears" (Hebrews 5:7) while His closest friends abandoned Him emotionally. This preceded the loneliness He would experience during His trials and crucifixion. At His arrest, "they all forsook Him and fled" (Mark 14:50). He had to confront His darkest hours alone. We know that God was always with Him. Intellectually we know that if we have God, we have all that we need. But it often seems like God is not enough! We need a human voice, a warm hug, eye contact, and reassurance. It may surprise us to know that Jesus also needed something tangible. Luke's account of Gethsemane includes a surprise visitation from heaven. "Then an angel appeared to Him from heaven, strengthening Him" (Luke 22:43).

If Jesus needed extra support in an agonizing situation, He knows we do too. He promises strength sufficient for our needs. And He can use us to provide strength to others when they hurt.

MRS. MARCIA HORNOK

Thank You for letting me come boldly to your throne of grace to find help in my time of need. Amen

Hidden Blessings

My soul, wait silently for God alone, for my expectation is from Him. Psalm 62:5 NKJ

There used to be a TV show called "Mama's Family." In one episode the main character, Thelma, tells her grandson about her oldest brother, Clyde, who loved to hunt. More than anything else, Clyde wanted a fifty-dollar rifle for his graduation from high school. Since Clyde was his father's favorite, he was sure he would get it. Graduation came, and Clyde opened the gift from his father—a Bible! He was so disgusted, he left home the next day and never came back. Many years later, after his father's death, Clyde cleaned out the attic and came across the Bible, still in its box. Leafing through it, he found a fifty-dollar bill. At this point in the show, the grandson asks Thelma, "Why didn't his dad tell him about the money?" Thelma answers, "Why didn't Clyde read the Bible? He could have had what he wanted all along, but it came in a different package than he expected, so he missed it."

When God gives us situations we'd rather not have, we should search for hidden blessings. God has a way of making our problems result in blessings. By the same token, when God seems not to answer prayer, I must not doubt His love or His power. His answer may come in a way I never expected. Rather than focus on what I expect God to do, I must concentrate on what He expects from me—my love and trust.

Mrs. Marcia Hornok

Lord, please enable me to see the good in grief as I yield my expectations up to you. Amen

This Little Light

For we are God's workmanship, created in Christ Jesus to do good works, which God prepared in advance for us to do.

Ephesians 2:10 NIV

I sat at the kitchen table, sipping a steaming cup of coffee, and staring with satisfaction down the hallway to our front entrance. My husband had just installed a stained-glass window in the sidelight of our front door. The window depicted a peacock, tail flowing and head turned. Blue, green and gold glass. Bevels outlined the entire window. As God's sunlight shone through, the colors came alive and rainbows danced on the walls. I made that beautiful window. Yes, me! I studied nine weeks in class; spent hundreds of dollars on supplies, honed my skills for a year, and spent months creating my window. I cut hundreds of pieces of glass by hand, ground them with a diamond grinder, foiled them in copper, and soldered them together. It's the most beautiful piece of stained glass I ever made. I don't say this to boast about my skills, but rather to boast about my Lord's creativity and magnificence.

I'm proud of my window, and I suppose I could take full credit for my workmanship. But the truth is, I am creative because He is creative. The colors dance on my wall because He created sunlight. He gave me the ability and desire to work with my hands. He created the majestic peacock copied into the pattern. He is awesome! It's not the window itself, but the creative process that brings Him glory. It's God's light shining through the window. And you—yes, you—are a beautiful creation of His workmanship when His light shines through you.

MRS. MARY ENGLUND MURPHY

Father, may your light always shine through me and may you be glorified in the process. Amen

Tables of Honor

For everyone who exalts himself will be humbled...
Luke 14:11a NIV

In Luke Chapter 14, Jesus was invited to a Pharisee's home for the Sabbath meal. Although this was common practice, the religious leaders were always plotting ways to find fault with Him. Jesus is perfectly aware of their attitudes (John 2: 24-25) and in this particular event He exposes their false views of popularity and success. Motivated by pride and selfishness, many dinner guests desired to have the best seats at the table (cf. Proverbs 25:6, 7). It is clear God is not impressed by outward appearances (1 Samuel 16:7; James 4:6), our status in society or the church. Jesus' mission was to preach the gospel to the needy and poor, those who could not repay. Contrast this to King David (2 Samuel 9:5-13) who extended his mercy and generosity to Mephibosheth, the grandson of Saul, one of his adversaries to the throne. Mephibosheth was given a place of honor at the King's table. David did not look upon him as a cripple or an outcast but as a person of value. The Pharisee's would have done well if they had followed David's example, a man after God's own heart.

FOOD FOR THOUGHT

1. Experts in management claim most people wear invisible signs saying, "Please make me feel important." Can we be successful with that attitude?
2. Read Philippians 2:1-16. How does God exalt the humble?
3. The religious leaders were more interested in sitting in the "right seats" than living the right kind of life before God.

Mrs. Lori Ciccanti

"Search me, O God, and know my heart; test me and know my anxious thoughts. See if there is any offensive way in me." (Psalm 139:23, 24) Amen

Papa Chón

How blessed is the man who fears the LORD, who greatly delights in His commandments. His descendants will be mighty on earth; the generation of the upright will be blessed.

Psalm 112:1-2 NASB

In the late 1890's, my great-grandfather, Galación Garza (Papa Chón) was led to the Lord by missionaries in northern Mexico. At this time missionaries were suffering persecution in Mexico. Papa Chón became a faithful Christian, even though his wife did not share his beliefs. His daughter Antonia, my grandmother, met Arturo Alemán around 1915. In 1917, Arturo accepted Jesus as his personal Savior at a revival campaign held in Del Valle, Texas. The night Arturo made his faith public, his father tried to go into the church and drag him out but was stopped by men outside the church. Arturo became a lay preacher. Later his family returned to Mexico. They told their son that due to his conversion they no longer had reason to maintain contact with him. After sixteen years however, they were reunited.

Arturo and Antonia married in 1919. Papa Arturo and Mama Toña had six children. The first died of meningitis as a toddler. One became a pastor; my father, Moses has been a part time music minister and the others have been faithful servants in the church. Papa Arturo and Mama Toña had seventeen grandchildren. Three are full time ministers and two are pastors' wives. Others are serving as elders, deacons, and in various ministries of the church. Forty great-grandchildren have been born. This generation includes faithful followers of Christ and one who is preparing to serve God in another country as a missionary. God has certainly honored Papa Chón's faithfulness!

Mrs. Karen Alemán Dishman

Jehovah God, may I be a faithful servant as my fathers have before me. Amen

In His Plans

> *"For I know the plans I have for you," declares the Lord, "plans to prosper you and not to harm you, plans to give you hope and a future. Then you will call upon me and come and pray to me, and I will listen to you."* Jeremiah 29:11-12 NIV

We had been in South Africa almost a year and still we were not where we wanted to be. My husband and I had received the challenge to go as missionaries to Namibia. Our hearts were filled with great anticipation and excitement as we landed in stunning Cape Town, South Africa. Our stay in this beautiful city was only to be until we could get our work permits to go to Namibia. After waiting 4 months, we finally got word that we had been denied work permits. We traveled to a town close to Namibia and tried again for permits. For the second time we were denied our work permits. What was the Lord saying to us? Did we miss His directions? What were His plans for us? We were so disappointed and cried out to God as to what He was saying to us. The answer was surprising but true. We were already in the place God wanted us to be. The town that we thought we would just be passing through was where God wanted us to stay.

We were thrilled as we saw the Lord open up many doors of ministry in hearts and lives of so many people he brought along our paths. My husband and I began to realize that sometimes God's plans are closer than we realize. We can make our plans, but God directs our steps.

MRS. JANICE UPTON

Thank you, Jesus, that your plans are so much better than my plans. Amen

Like My Dog

...yet the dogs eat of the crumbs which fall from their masters' table. Matthew 15:27 KJV

Our home has been graced with the presence of a bundle of mischief by the name of Ranger. He is a rambunctious terrier with sparkling eyes and a tail that is always on the move. Although he's a family dog, Ranger's singular devotion proves that my husband alone is his true master. It is at my husband's feet that Ranger will reside in the quiet moments of the evening. When he rises to leave the room, Ranger will follow. And when he is not at home, Ranger is longing for his return. Oh, that I would be so with my Master! Lord, help my devotion to be singularly yours. May I cherish your presence, sit at your feet, follow where you lead. And when I sense your absence, may I be found seeking you. Lord, make me like my dog!

But there is a particular trait in Ranger that has perplexed me. Although he loves the presence of his master, yet his devotion seems to be forgotten as soon as the front door is opened. The opportunity for "adventure" overcomes him, and out the door he will bolt, away from the comforts of his master. That which he is so intent on enjoying one moment, he will flee from the next. At this sight, I must sadly see my own tendency. Although I have loved the sweet fellowship of my Savior, yet how often will I be lured away from Him by my sin? I cry with the hymn writer:

> *"Prone to wander, Lord I feel it, Prone to leave the God I love! Here's my heart, Lord, Take and seal it, Seal it for Thy courts above!"*

Mrs. Jan Kimbro

Lord, help me to hunger for You and to never stray. Amen

God's Inscrutability

> *For who has known the mind of the Lord? Or who has become His counselor?* Romans 11:34 NKJ

For the first anniversary of 9/11, I organized an evangelistic outreach for our church. We rented a park pavilion and advertised a free breakfast, inviting all the fire fighters and police officers in our area. We prepared for 75 visitors. That morning it rained for the first time in two months, and the temperature set a record low for that day of 53 degrees. No visitors came. The two fire fighters who did attend got called to a fire right after the flag ceremony.

I know of a minister's wife who finally conceived a baby after nine years of infertility. One week before the due date, the baby strangled in her cord and died. Sometimes we simply can't understand what God is doing or why. He is inscrutable to us. Inscrutability means that God does not have to explain Himself. If I could interpret Him or figure Him out, I would be His equal—how ludicrous (and prideful) is that? Often He does reveal possible reasons for our trials, but that should not be my focus. It took a period of mental illness to teach King Nebuchadnezzar that no one can say to God, "What have You done?" (Daniel 4:34-35). Job learned it after losing everything dear except his critical wife (Job 40:1-5). God answered Job's questions with interrogation not explanation, teaching us that God does not have to defend Himself. Even if my adverse circumstances seem inexplicable and senseless, I can trust God anyhow. He knows what He's doing in my life, and that means I don't have to.

Mrs. Marcia Hornok

O Lord, You are all-wise, all-loving, and all-good—that's all I need to know. Amen

Daddy, Will It Hurt?

...I will never leave thee... Hebrews 13:5 KJV

We sat in the surgical waiting room watching as our little Jessica played happily with the hospital toys. She seemed the picture of health. But the doctors had explained that her condition required major surgery, and that the recovery would be painful. Reggie called Jessie to come sit on his lap. "Now darling," his voice sounded calm, "the nurse will be here in a minute to get you ready, just like we talked about." "Okay, Daddy," her tone was quiet and serious. "Daddy?" "Yes, Darlin.'" "Will it hurt when I wake up?" "Yes, Darlin." She paused. "A lot?" He pulled her in closer. "Yes, Darlin'" We sat still and quiet. Hours later we were at the bedside of a different little girl. Her face was swollen and pale, and her brow was furrowed in pain. This was worse than I had imagined. What must she think of our love? This little girl trusted us. How in the midst of this pain could she understand why? Reggie bent over to kiss her. "I'm right here," he whispered. Her pained expression melted and she smiled sweetly. "I know, Daddy."

Then I realized—she didn't need to understand why. It hit me: "As a Father pitieth his children" and "except ye become as little children." How our hearts pitied our little one, but the overwhelming ache was but a shadow of the compassion our Lord has for us in our times of pain. We can trust Him. He understands why and that's enough!

Mrs. Jan Kimbro

Dear Father, give me the faith of a child who trusts You even in pain. May I hear your voice, "I will never leave you," and may I gaze lovingly into your face and reply, "I know." Amen

Transformed Inside and Out

> *I beseech you therefore, brethren, by the mercies of God, that you present your bodies a living sacrifice, holy, acceptable to God, which is your reasonable service. And do not be conformed to this world, but be transformed by the renewing of your mind, that you may prove what is that good and acceptable and perfect will of God.*
> Romans 12:1-2 NKJ

I have a dream. It is to buy and renovate a Victorian house. My dream house would have a wrap-around porch and a turret with quaint round rooms. It would be painted in coordinating pastel shades with lovely gingerbread and scrollwork, and a white picket fence would border a carpet of grass. The inside would have high molded ceilings, stained-glass windows, and other decorative details. The winding oak staircase would lead to bedrooms filled with antique furniture and lovely handmade quilts. There are two ways to make an old house look as glorious as my dream home. The first is to make superficial repairs, do a thorough cleaning, and paint the walls. The second is to check the electrical and plumbing, examine for wood rot, inspect the roof, siding, and foundation, to determine what internal improvements need to be made. Sometimes an old structure needs to be gutted in order to make it strong and stable on the inside, not just pretty on the outside.

My dream reminds me of the renovation God wants to do in our lives. He wants to gut us by taking away all that is potentially destructive to our lives. He wants to rebuild us from the inside out with His own godly character so our lives will reflect and glorify Him.

Mrs. Mary Englund Murphy

Dear Lord, may you transform me into one who always glorifies You. Amen

Jesus, Carry Me

I have made you and I will carry you; I will sustain you and I will rescue you. Isaiah 46:4b NIV

During a very painful time in my life, I found it difficult to pray. I could not put my thoughts and longings into words. It was then I thought of the "Footprints" poem. In the story of the poem a man notices two sets of prints are in the sand as His Savior walks with him on the journey of life. Then when life was most difficult and filled with sorrow, there is only one set of prints. The man asked Jesus the meaning of this. Jesus' answer was, "During your times of trial and suffering, when you see only one set of footprints, it was then that I carried you."

I decided to embrace this truth. I began to pray this simple prayer; "Jesus, Carry Me." I felt the arms of Jesus around me, I knew He was with me. I knew He was carrying me and would walk with me through this dark and painful time. Other Bible verses blessed me in this journey: Isaiah 41:10b says, "I will strengthen you and help you; I will uphold you with my righteous right hand." Deuteronomy 33:27 reminds us that "The eternal God is your refuge and underneath are the everlasting arms" (of the Lord). Armed with the Word of God and resting in the arms of my Savior, I found sweet comfort and peace.

Mrs. Shirley Ann Unrau

God of the outstretched arms, thank you that You wait for us to crawl into your arms so that You can carry us through the storms of life. We trust You with our pains and struggles, for You are Almighty God, Prince of Peace. Amen

Techno-burdened

Come to me, all you who are weary and burdened, and I will give you rest. Take my yoke upon you and learn from me, for I am gentle and humble in heart, and you will find rest for your souls.

Matthew 11:28, 29 NIV

The world today is not a place of rest. We are bombarded by communication gadgets that long to control our time--cell phones that ring or text us continually, email, the internet, TV, games--all beg for our time and attention. Many have become essentials in our daily work and "must do" in our down time. But God is still calling us to Himself. He desires for us to pursue Him, spend time with Him, hear His voice and read his Text message. How can we "be holy as He is holy" if we are not seeking Him? In Him we find our edge to overcome, our rest, our restoration, our hope, our strength, and our power to choose the holy above the unholy. The tyranny of the urgent calls us to be busy doing, but God calls us to rest in Him so that the urgent does not consume us.

God calls us to be in the world, but not of the world. Light-bearers bringing light to a dark, desperate world that is floundering, fearful, and tired. Choosing to spend time with God and learn from Him enables us to live above the fray, to make wise choices, and reflect His light to a hurting world. It reminds us that we are called to live holy and love God rather than the world. As we pursue Him, the draw of the world grows dimmer. The words from the old gospel song become our song, "I'd rather have Jesus than anything this world affords today."

Mrs. Charlotte Ford

Dear Father, may I choose to hear from You above all others today. Amen

Me! A Preacher's Wife?

Faithful is he that calleth you... I Thessalonians 5:24 KJV

My husband was not a pastor when we got married. The Lord called him to preach five years and two kids later. Growing up as a preacher's kid, I had decided long ago that I did not want to raise my kids in that "fish bowl" existence. The day Jim told me God had called him to preach, I rebelled. Shamefully, my exact words to him were, "Fine. You can be a preacher, but you might as well look for another wife because I won't be a preacher's wife." We went through months of turmoil. I kept rebelling. Jim kept praying. In fact, more than once, I caught my husband at the church, on his knees crying out to the Lord on my behalf. God could have brought some horrible circumstance into my life to draw my heart back to Him. But He didn't. He loved me back through my sweet husband and precious children. He loved me by showing himself faithful when I was faithless. The day came when I surrendered to His will.

It is thirty-two years later. I am a pastor's wife that LOVES being a pastor's wife! This role has its challenges, but what blessings I would have missed if I had stayed in rebellion against His plan for my life. If you are struggling with this role, please accept God's will. Maybe you didn't sign up for this, but I assure you that if you are married to a man who has been called to preach... you HAVE been called to be a pastor's wife.

MRS. VONNA S. DOWNS

Father, cause my heart to accept the journey You have planned for me. Amen

An Attitude of Contentment

...for I have learned to be content whatever the circumstances.
Philippians 4:11 NIV

An attitude of contentment is one that Paul tells Christians is learned. It obviously is not something that comes naturally. Discontentment reveals dissatisfaction with and a distrust of God. No matter the trial or tribulation that you are facing, there is a way to learn to be content through it. Our attitude of contentment is not only a personal area of growth but is also a great witness to the lost. It shows our trust and faith in the God of the universe and displays His reliability to His people.

I have been a missionary in the Middle East, the wife of a seminary student, experienced times of great marital difficulties, seen my plans falter with a surprise pregnancy, and struggled through personal times of depression. Yet I have never failed to see the hand of God sustain me. When I am content...whatever my lot...the grace of God seems much greater. He has taught this child contentment, and He can teach you as well, if you will let Him. Hymn-writer Horatio Spafford wrote *It is well with my soul* after the death of his four daughters. The words of this hymn have been a great ministry to my spirit on countless occasions. I encourage you to pick up a hymnal or download the words and music from the Internet and sing this song of surrender to the Lord.

Mrs. Courtney Chesney

Father, though my trials seem to overwhelm me, please bring contentment to my spirit through surrendering myself to You. Amen

A Senseless Mission?

Many are the plans in a man's heart, but it is the LORD's purpose that prevails. Proverbs 19:21 NIV

Ernest Gordon, serving with British troops during World War II, was captured in Southeast Asia and lived in prisoner of war camps for three and one-half years. He became one of the 60,000 POW's forced to build 250 miles of railroad and the bridge over the River Kwai. In his book, To End All Wars, Gordon wrote, "If I had learned to trust Jesus at all, I had to trust Him here." After two years in captivity, the POW's who had embraced Christianity held a worship service on Christmas day. When they sang the closing hymn, "Good Christian Men, Rejoice," air raid sirens began to wail. In the distance, they heard a rumble. As the sound increased, they realized it might be a US plane taking photographs. This encouraged their hearts and they sang, "Rejoice! Rejoice!" as lustily and loudly as they could. Afterward, a fellow POW said he wondered if the crew of that plane "had any idea what they meant to us."

Perhaps the flight crew had complained about the senseless mission they had to fly on Christmas, never knowing what a symbol of hope it had been to hundreds of POW's that day. How many of our own "senseless missions" do we complain about? *Why do I have to help clean the church? I wish I didn't have to visit the nursing home this week. Can't someone else tend the nursery?* God has His purposes, inscrutable to us. We will never know on earth all the positive effects we had on others when we carried out His "senseless" assignments.

MRS. MARCIA HORNOK

Father, I accept whatever plans You have for me today. Amen

Numbering Our Days

So teach us to number our days, that we may apply our hearts unto wisdom.
Psalm 90:12 KJV

When we set out to describe one who is diligent in their studies we say that they "apply themselves." So it must be in our pursuit of wisdom. We must apply ourselves, our whole hearts to it. There is an urgency that comes to one who has learned to number her days. But we must be careful to respond to this sense of urgency in faith and not in the flesh. The real task is not that which is seen but rather that which is unseen. Applying our hearts unto wisdom is an act of faith, not of sight. The passage doesn't say that we are to apply our hearts unto outward service or good works but that we must first apply ourselves to inward understanding or wisdom. This inward work of sanctification must be our focus. We must apply ourselves unto Christ, the embodiment of all wisdom. When we truly number our days, it is to Him we will run. Faith will draw us to the one who can make our service effective, to the one who can produce in us unfeigned fruit.

When we feel the urgency of the brevity of this life, it will cause us to flee from hypocrisy and outward conformity. Instead we will pursue real and lasting fruit that can only be produced by looking away to our Savior, by fleeing to Him, and by sitting at His feet! It is to this wisdom that we must apply our hearts. Life is a vapor; how urgently we need to know the presence of Christ!

Mrs. Jan Kimbro

Father, teach us to number our days so that we may apply our hearts unto You! Amen

A Baby with a Story to Tell

> *We will not hide them from their children; we will tell the next generation the praiseworthy deeds of the LORD, his power, and the wonders he has done.* Psalm 78:4 NIV

For the second time, at thirty-one weeks into my pregnancy, I was ambulanced to a facility where they could properly care for a preterm baby in their Neonatal Intensive Care Unit. This time my pre-eclampsia symptoms were severe enough to mandate delivery in order to save my life. After several hours of constant labor pain, I was whisked into the operating room for an emergency c-section. "Code blue" rang through the halls at 3:00 a.m. A team of doctors and nurses worked furiously to deliver and resuscitate my baby, whose heartbeat had stopped. After six attempts, they were about to give up, shaking their heads in silence. With one final attempt, we heard the most beautiful cry we've ever heard, although it sounded more like a little kitten whimpering. I later learned that I also had placental abruption, which meant the baby was not getting oxygen or nourishment. Women with pre-eclampsia or placental abruption don't always survive. God saved me. God saved my baby. He gave her that breath of life. That is quite a story I have now to tell of God's power over life and death. I hope my daughter will tell her story to future generations, a story of the wonders God has done in her life.

Do you have a story to tell? Has God shown His power to you in an undeniable way? Then don't deny Him. Tell your story.

MRS. DAISY WONG

> *Lord, give me boldness and courage to tell of your strength and your wonderful works. Amen*

What Shall I Wear Today?

...clothed me with garments of salvation and arrayed me in a robe of righteousness. Isaiah 61:10b NIV

How often we ladies seem to have to face the decision of what to pull out of our wardrobes! And, usually, it only comes down to choosing what is most appropriate for the occasion. (Or, sometimes which one is cleanest, least wrinkled---and still fits us!) As to our spiritual apparel, we Christians have already been clothed in the righteousness of Christ (Isaiah 61:10; 2 Corinthians 5:21; Galatians 3:27) because we're justified.

However, when it comes to our sanctification, we are commanded to put on various traits already provided for us in our wardrobes. And we must choose *daily* to put these on. (See one of the "catalogs" in Ephesians 4:20-32.) The fashions of the day should be *compassion* (the same as Christ has shown to us), *kindness* (in both words and deeds—those neighbors may be carrying a heavier burden than we are facing), *gentleness* (sometimes shown by simply lending a listening ear), *patience* (even in those long lines and with those demanding persons), and *love* (which seems to be described as an eloquent sash for binding together all these virtues, so very much needed in this world of disunity). (See the descriptive "catalog" of Colossians 3:12-17.) Today, as we must be on display before so many (believers and *non*-believers), let us rely on the Holy Spirit to keep us "radiant, without spot or wrinkle" (Ephesians 5:27). Then these onlookers should be able to see what a great Designer our God is!

MRS. CAROLYN LYON

Lord, may I today make the right choices in my spiritual apparel for every occasion. Amen

Mary's Heart Cry

...be it unto me according to thy word. Luke 1:38 KJV

The Virgin Mary surely had hopes and dreams. What young woman, engaged to a man she loved and respected, would not have her heart filled with youthful plans? She awaited a lovely wedding, a honeymoon, and then building a family with her new husband. Yet on the day of the Angel's pronouncement, these plans were all changed. Mary was called upon to sacrifice her dreams. The reputation that any godly young woman would naturally have nourished was to be forfeited, the public wedding celebration canceled. Even the trust of her fiancée would be jeopardized. Yet what is the response of our young heroine? It was faith that produced a happy submission to the will of her Father. Oh, may we learn from her example!

How we hope and dream toward each new stage of life, yet where is the will of our Father in all our plans? Do we have a high and honorable view of God's will that makes plans of our own seem insignificant? Do we really trust in the wisdom and goodness of our God? Do we value His kingdom more than the kingdom of our own little life? Mary's faith in God caused her mind to be freed from thoughts of self. Her dreams were pushed out of the way, but she gladly accepted what the angel told her. Her joy spilled over as she testified, "My soul doth magnify the Lord, and my spirit hath rejoiced in God my Savior!"

Mrs. Jan Kimbro

Lord, give me this joy! Turn me from self-willed pursuits that I may delight to do thy bidding! Like Mary, may my heart cry "be it unto me according to THY word!" Amen

With Eyes to See

All things were made by him; and without him was not any thing made that was made. John 1:3 KJV

It is spring as I write this, and all around me growing things are awakening from their sleep. The colors are vibrant and rich. Right before our eyes, and seemingly overnight, trees bud and bloom; grass turns green. But I wonder: what if I could not see these things? When we lived near Gardner-Webb University, I often drove by the campus in Boiling Springs, North Carolina, and saw blind students crossing the streets near their campus. How sharp they were in maneuvering around campus and how attuned to their surroundings they were without physical sight!

How about our sight? How well do we see? I had a child in school that was dressed very poorly and looked sad each day. As I talked with her I discovered that she walked to school every day. My daughter was about her size, and I began keeping some sweaters and extra shirts for her to put on. I also gave her snacks. From my principal I found out that the family was living in a car not far from school. We began getting things together for them and trying to find a place for them to live but, before that could happen, one day the car was gone. What I had seen was very hard for me. And even though I tried, I could not fix it. We need more than sight to meet the needs of a hurting world. We need insight!

MRS. BETSY MCSWAIN

Help us Lord, to see needs and to let our "want to" match our "ought to." Amen

Discovering God's Wisdom

"For my thoughts are not your thoughts,"...says the LORD.
Isaiah 55:8 NKJ

Tiny children are so funny as they brag about their dads. We have all probably heard them making such comparisons as: "My pop's smarter than your pop" or "My dad's better than your dad." Children love to admire and trust their dads. They think their earthly fathers can do anything.

But how do we, as Christians, think of our Heavenly Father? When we are troubled, if we could think clearly about how smart our Heavenly Father is (after all, He created all knowledge), many of our misgivings about life would take on a different perspective. How often do you think about how intelligent and wise God is? He is the wisest Father anyone could ever have, and He wants to listen to us through our prayers and advise us through the Bible's wisdom. James bragged about his Heavenly Father's wisdom and His desire to pass it on to us (1:5): "If any of you lacks wisdom, let him ask of God, who gives to all liberally and without reproach, and it will be given to him."

Mrs. Janet Miller

Father, it is our desire to honor You with every part of our being. Help us to gain biblical wisdom so that our lives will bring honor to You. Amen

Growing Up—Disappointed

...for you are still carnal. For where there are envy, strife, and divisions among you, are you not carnal and behaving like mere men? I Corinthians 3:3 NKJ

Today's writing assignment for my students was, "Explain how disappointment can have a good side." This is always an interesting writing prompt. How a student responds is a quick measure of his maturity level. One student wrote, "There is nothing good about disappointment. It is all BAD, BAD, BAD!" Several others wrote that disappointment was just something you had to get through and eventually something good would happen that would make you forget what you didn't get. Only one student wrote that you *can* learn from your disappointment: you might learn that you didn't really need what you wanted or what you wanted was not a good thing for you.

I like to think I'm more mature than my eighth grade pupils but sadly, many times my response to a disappointment is exactly like my students' responses. Sometimes I'm so angry and hurt my only thought is, "This is so BAD." Or I'll take the old "grit my teeth and bear it" approach, suffer through it, and concentrate on something fun in the future. However, if I am really growing in Christ, I am able to reflect on my disappointment. I can ask, "Did I really need what I was wanting? Would this really have been good for me?" I can't be growing if I only see disappointment as bad or something to get past. Each disappointment is an opportunity brought into my life by a loving heavenly Father. It is an opportunity to trust Him for what I really need.

MRS. SUZAN MOYER

God, give me an understanding heart to see the good I can learn from disappointments. Amen

Times & Seasons

January Stillness

Be still, and know that I am God. Psalm 46:10a NIV

What is your favorite month of the year? Several years ago, January would have been last on my list. Back then the thought of cold weather caused me to cringe down to my wool-socked toes. January—and the winter it typifies--loomed like a bleak, blustery, colorless month that could only be endured. I considered getting in on the bears' hibernation schedule. What changed? Maybe it was getting married in January. Suddenly there was a permanent bright spot on the calendar at that time each year. Whatever the reason, January does have its charms.

After Christmas and the New Year holidays, life resumes with the hustle and bustle of daily routines—family, work, and church responsibilities. Overall, though, winter whispers a quiet simplicity that hushes the land, a brisk stillness that can be seen in bare tree branches and blankets of snow. It's as if nature has paused for a moment. God invites us to pause as well. We may be reminiscing about the holidays we've just gone through, but we're also remaining grateful for His countless blessings every day of the year. In Him we can glean hope for the days and years ahead. When our schedules slow down or the weather brings everything to a standstill, we have a chance to stop and just think--often a rarity in our busy days.

Mrs. Alison Bryant

Quiet my busy thoughts, Lord, so that I can focus only on who You are. Amen

God's Splendorous Love

A friend loves at all times... Proverbs 17:17a NKJ

"Love is a many-splendored thing. . . ," "I'm in the mood for Love," and "April Love." Ahhh, LOVE! Love songs play on radio stations. TV stations show classic love stories. You know Valentine's Day is near when love is in advertisements, at the mall, and even in the grocery store. You see hearts, lace, Cupids, and, yes, lots of chocolate! What do you think of when you think of Valentine's Day?Probably romantic love. But the Bible tells us there are three different kinds of love: *Phileo* love, the friendship love; Eros love, the erotic love; and *Agape* love, God's love. To quote another song title: "What the world needs now is love." It needs the *agape* kind of love, God's love, and it needs it not only on Valentine's Day but every day of the year.

Why not call several people just to tell them that you love them? What about reaching out to a neighbor you never speak to?How about the elderly in your church?They may not have anyone who thinks of them on their birthdays or special occasions. How about showing special attention to a child whose parents are divorced? Why not treat a single parent and his or her child to McDonald's or a family-friendly movie? Beloved ones, when we practice God's perfect love, we will want to reach out to those who are without love. Can't you just hear Jesus say, "Lovest thou Me?" When we love Him, we'll show and share our love with others 365 days a year.

MRS. GEORGIA M. SAWHOOK

Lord, help us to show your love to others as you so unselfishly showed your love to us on Calvary. Amen

When Easter Comes

But God commendeth his love toward us, in that, while we were yet sinners, Christ died for us. Romans 5:8 KJV

What is your favorite holiday?In a little book of children's prayers, a little girl named Ginny wrote this prayer."Dear God, please put another holiday between Christmas and Easter. There is nothing good in there now."

It can seem like a long time (of cold winter) between Christmas and Easter, but Easter eventually comes. My favorite part of the season is Holy Week because of what took place so long ago in Jerusalem. It comes even more alive for me as I think about seeing Jerusalem from the Mount of Olives as my husband and I toured the Holy Land last year. We walked down the stone steps to the Eastern Gate. We walked along the city streets of old Jerusalem and felt Him close to us. As I left the temple area and stood in the courtyard where the statue of Peter, the maiden and the cock were, tears came to my eyes. I thought about this place and the life that had been crucified for me. What an impact this had on my life!

Whether you have been able to visit the Holy Land yet or not, may we each reflect today on what happened there almost two thousand years ago—the great love and sacrifice of Jesus as He died on a hill outside Jerusalem.

MRS. BETSY MCSWAIN

O God, may we take time to reflect on what You did for us at Calvary and the new life we have in You. Amen

HE IS RISEN!

He is not here: for he is risen, as he said. Come, see the place where the Lord lay. Matthew 28:6 KJV

Praise God! Jesus said, "Because I live you, too, shall live." Oh the blessed hope. Isn't Resurrection morning such a special time? The grass is a brighter green, the clouds are whiter, the sky is bluer, the birds sing louder, and you have a zip in your step. It's so exciting. What was it like on the first Easter morning? The disciples had lost all hope. Mary had gone to the tomb to prepare the body for the burial with spices and with a sad heart. She walked slowly as she approached the tomb. There she found an angel standing guard. What happened? Why was the stone removed? And then the angel told her, "He is not here. HE IS RISEN!"

Her feet ran swiftly as she went to tell the others. Did they ask: Are you crazy, Mary? What have you been drinking so early in the morning? They doubted but just to make sure, Peter and John ran to see for themselves. And they saw what Mary had seen. Hallelujah! Jesus is not there. HE HAS RISEN! Jesus is alive and sitting at the right hand of God the Father to rule and reign with Him. From heaven, Jesus defends us daily. He hears and answers our prayers. He comforts us. And just think that if I (or you) had been the only one in the world, He would have died for me (or for you). Rejoice and be glad, dear hearts. Our Savior and Shepherd is alive and waiting for us. He's preparing our home so that we have a place to live forever with Him.

MRS. GEORGIA M. SAWHOOK

I thank you, Lord, for being willing to die for me—and for not letting death defeat You so that I can live forever with You. Amen

Changing Seasons

Jesus Christ the same yesterday, and to day, and for ever.
Hebrews 13:5 KJV

Autumn brings us another time of reflection. It's refreshing because the hot and dry summer is past and the upcoming fall is becoming evident in the cooler mornings and less humid evenings. My ideal weather conditions for heaven are 70 degrees, sunny, and a breeze. (Of course, I know that whatever the weather conditions in heaven are, they will be perfect, right?) Then we veer into the future with the beautiful fall season in its entire splendor. The leaves turn vibrant colors, the air becomes crisp and cool in the day and chilly in the night. And there's that certain smell about autumn--the falling leaves--the garden flowers and vegetables withering and dying on the plants--the cornstalks drying. There are the beautiful colors of pumpkins, gourds, and squash gracing our tables and landscapes. The end of one season while preparing to go into another. From one season to another there are changes and more changes. Nothing ever stays the same.

But praise God! There is Someone who NEVER changes: our Savior, God the Father, and the Holy Spirit. "For I am the LORD, I change not… " (Malachi 3:6 KJV). In this world of technology and changing seasons, it's a comfort to know that Jesus is always the same. He hasn't changed just because it's the 21st century. So, in the changing seasons of our lives—remember that Jesus Christ is our Constant. He's always there. And He never changes.

MRS. GEORGIA M. SAWHOOK

Dear Lord, what a wonderful comfort to know that even though the seasons change and we change, You are a changeless God. Amen

Love Came Down at Christmas

Ye shall find the babe wrapped in swaddling clothes, lying in a manger. Luke 2:12b KJV

As my husband and I traveled to Bethlehem last year with Chowan University Group, I was disturbed as we drove to the guarded wall. We saw the guards with guns as we went through the gate. Then on to a place where some believe Jesus was born. There we worshiped together in the small cave. This was the birth town of the "Prince of Peace" and yet today there is no peace.

I reflected on a Christmas gone by when I was teaching second grade. I let the children share what they wanted for Christmas. Then one child asked me what I wanted for Christmas. I said that I would love to have a doll. Most of them thought that it was funny for an adult to want a doll. On the last day before the holidays, Ashley brought me a tiny gift. She wanted me to open it before she left that day. So I did. She was excited as I carefully looked inside and found a tiny doll dressed in white. I almost cried. I hugged and thanked her. She was so thrilled that I liked it. (Her mother told me later how she had diligently shopped for her teacher because Santa might run out of dolls before he got to the big people). I still have that little doll, for it is such a sweet expression of love at Christmas. As we approach this time of sharing gifts and our love, may we remember that Jesus, the Babe in Bethlehem, was the greatest gift of Love.

Mrs. Betsy Swain

Our Father, may we sense anew the great love You gave the world at Christmas. Amen

A Great Light

The people walking in darkness have seen a great light; on those living in the land of the shadow of death a light has dawned.
Isaiah 9:2 NIV

This is the reason we celebrate the marvelous birth of Jesus--He has finally come! Emmanuel is with us. Those who are walking in darkness and death can choose life and freedom in Jesus. This is the good news we have to share with those we come in contact with who are dead men and women walking. Jesus will light up your life. He will give you abundant life.

I met Rena at a church where my husband was preaching in South Africa. She was so depressed, feeling out of place because she was a single mother with two children, and most of the church members were married couples. I asked the Lord to show me what I should share with her from the Word of God. The Holy Spirit directed me to the passage in Matthew 26:7 dealing with the woman with the alabaster box. This was exactly what Rena needed to hear. She could be set free. She could be forgiven. Rena became a changed person that day. She told everyone she met what Jesus had done for her. Her favorite words were "I am so excited with Jesus, and the best is yet to come." Her old boyfriends would come around and ask her what she had been doing. Her answer to them was, "I have met a man and His name is JESUS and He has changed me." Then she would say to them, "Would you like Jesus in your life?"

MRS.JANICE UPTON

Dear Jesus, help my life to be a light to others. Amen

Happy Birthday, Jesus!

Thanks be unto God for his unspeakable gift.

II Corinthians 9:15 KJV

Happy Birthday, to You! Happy Birthday, to You! Happy Birthday, dear Jesus! Happy Birthday to You! Oh, what a joyful time of year! I just love it! People tend to be kinder or smile more (when they don't, I give them a bigger smile :). The music in the stores is so cheerful and makes you feel like singing. The generosity of folks is more evident. The atmosphere of Christmas is felt and seen everywhere. "Peace on earth, good will to men." Something BIG is coming. NO! It's not Santa Claus. Yes, it's our Lord and Savior Jesus Christ's birthday.

Jesus made His appearance on this earth many years ago. On that night a bright star shone in the skies to announce this holy occasion. The star announcing that the "star of David" was here, ready to become the Savior of all mankind. The Father sent His Son to meet the fate He knew He must meet, in order to fulfill prophecy and provide the needed sacrifice—a sinless sacrifice. He was that most holy, perfect One. He did this all for you and me. It warms my heart to realize that the God of all creation loved us so much that "He was not willing that any should perish, but that all would come to repentance" through His Son. Christmas is Jesus' birthday—His first coming to this earth as a man. Someday He *will* come again. His second coming will be to take those of us who have claimed Him as our Lord and Savior. Until then, Happy Birthday, Jesus!

Mrs. Georgia M. Sawhook

Dear God in heaven, THANK YOU SO MUCH for your precious Gift, for MY Jesus. Amen

Christmas Vows

"I am the Lord's servant," Mary answered. "May it be to me as you have said." Then the angel left her. Luke 1:38 NIV

Oh, the joys of a little child and the magic of the Christmas season. I remember how I would count the days before Christmas. It always seemed like an eternity. Now it seems like yesterday was Christmas and it is back again today. Maturity can change your perspective on time, but sweet memories remain unchanged and cherished. There is nothing like the aromas that my mother could make come out of the kitchen at Christmas time. Cakes in the oven, turkey and ham baking, all kinds of special dishes made all things bright and beautiful to my little eyes. The intoxicating smell of the cedar Christmas tree was unforgettable throughout the house.

Christmas Day is not only special to me because of those childhood memories but it is precious to me because it is my wedding day! JC and I were married on December 25, 1969. We chose to be married on Christ's birthday because we wanted to give our lives together as gifts to our Heavenly Father in remembrance of His one and only Son coming to earth. It has been almost 40 years now since we said to the Lord "we want to be your servants–use us as you will." God has graciously led us on our journey with Him and blessed us with three wonderful children and six delightful grandchildren. Now we are busy making magnificent memories for our children and grandchildren at Christmas time. It is a pleasure because the best is yet to come.

Mrs. Janice Upton

Dear Jesus what a delight and privilege it is to be your servant. Use me today for your glory. Amen

Christmas at Our House

Glory to God in the highest, And on earth peace, goodwill toward men!
Luke 2:14 NKJV

We wanted to teach our children the real reason for Christmas. They were not taught about Santa Claus (we call him The Big Red Lie). We stressed that God loves to give gifts to us, and He gave Jesus. Since we love each other, we give gifts to each other. Every evening from Thanksgiving to Christmas, for our family devotions we would read Luke 2:1-14. When we came to verse 7, we'd sing "Away in a Manger." At verse 8 we'd sing "While Shepherds Watched Their Flocks." At verse 14 the children would shout, "Glory to God in the highest, and on earth peace, goodwill towards men." Then we sang "Joy to the World." By December 25, the kids had committed to memory the entire selection of Luke 2:1-14.

When people asked our children, "What did Santa bring you?" They would reply, "Nothing. But Mom and Dad gave us gifts for Jesus' birthday." We usually opened our gifts the day before Christmas, so that Christmas day our whole focus was on worshipping the Lord. That was Christmas at our house.

Mrs. Betty Mick

Lord, help us to keep a pure Christmas, and give us grace to honor You in our special remembrance of the birth of Jesus. Amen

A Keeper of Promises

Let us hold fast the profession of our faith without wavering; (for he is faithful that promised;) Hebrews 10:23 KJV

Happy New Year!

Isn't the Lord wonderful to give us new beginnings, not only every day but every year? It seems like it's a clean slate and we immediately start to write on it. We may not call them resolutions, but many of us make new commitments, attempt new diets and exercise programs, set new goals, decide to adopt a healthier lifestyle, and promise to read God's Word through in a year. Don't forget: we also want to make every day more special in our prayer time with Him. Great goals!

But the problem with us is that we're all just plain old humans. And no matter how hard we try or how sincere our promises are, we DON'T always keep them, do we? Unlike us, there is one Promise Keeper who kept all His promises. Yes, you guessed it. God's Word is full of them: "Every promise in the Book is mine--every chapter, every verse, every line." Have you heard that children's song? Be assured that you are in good hands with Jesus because He keeps ALL His promises (even when we fail to keep ours). What a comfort!

MRS. GEORGIA M. SAWHOOK

Thank you, Lord, for being our Promise Keeper. We know we can trust You. You never fail us and You're ALWAYS there. Amen

Biographies

Diane Bakk, MN: along with her husband Jeff and 4 children, has called Vision of Glory Lutheran Ch home for the past 25 yrs; directs children's musicals and leads music teams for the church's weekly family production; also home educates her children, teaches music for her local home school co-op and instructs several private piano students.

Charlotte Boaz, CO: Husband Pastor John Boaz; graduated SMU nursing school; served as a Send Missionary in Japan until 1970; an active nurse since 1975; best yrs as Hospice nurse in Hawaii 1990-2000. Presently lives in Colorado Springs, CO.

Virginia Bonnette, GA: Husband Pastor Elmer "Del" Bonnette; 4 adult children: Joel, Jonathan, Eulanne and Freida; BA, Columbia Bible Col, Columbia, SC; Master's Degree, N GA Col, Dahlonega, GA; Clarkesville Bapt Ch, Clarkesville, GA; served with her husband as Southern Bapt Ch and then in churches in SC and GA.

Alison Bryant, NM: Husband Pastor David Bryant, P Blodgett Street Bapt Ch, Carlsbad, NM; they have enjoyed serving churches since 1994 in youth, educ., and worship ministry; Bachelor's Degree in social work, Hardin-Simmons U, Abilene, Texas: Master's Degree in Christian social work, Southwestern Bapt Theo Sem, Fort Worth, TX; www.alisonbryantwrites.com.

Margie Campbell, HI: Husband Rev. Bruce Campbell, pastor, Grace Community Ch, an Ev Free Church, Kailua Kona, Hawaii; they have ministered since church planting there in 1990; currently the women's ministry director; previously ministered in Honolulu and in CA; graduate of Chaffey College in Alta Loma, CA; 4 sons; Jason, Brian, Ben, and Joseph.

Courtney Chesney, GA: Husband Rev. Barry Chesney, Baptist Minister and PhD candidate; one son, expecting second child in 09; BA in Psychology/Political Science, Dallas Bapt U; currently a student at Southern Bapt Theol Sem working toward a Master's Degree in Biblical Counseling; served as a missionary to the Middle East with International Mission Bd of SBC; published in Voices of the Faithful by Beth Moore; serving at First Baptist Woodstock, GA.

Lori Ciccanti, DE: Husband Pastor Lou Ciccanti; mother of three children, one who is autistic. She belongs to The Bread of Life Ministries Association and is the editor of Aaron's Rod Newsletter—an outreach ministry inspiring children of God with disabilities to blossom using the gifts God has given them; Graduate, Liberty Bapt Home Bible Inst.

Becky Daman, WA: Husband Glenn is Director of the Center for Leadership Development and has written three books for small church pastors; pastor's wife for 21 yrs; an active leader of the women's ministries in each of the churches that her husband has served. Currently Becky is serving in Stevenson First Bapt Ch in Stevenson, Washington where her husband is SR Pastor.

Karen A. Dishman, OH: Husband Rev. R. Wayne Dishman, Pastor First Baptist Ch, Perrysburg, OH; 1 daughter—Leah, sons—Truett & Taylor; A.S. Bluefield Col; Trustee-Int'l Mission Bd, SBC 1991-1999; Officer-Recording Secretary; Women's Ministry Coordinator and Bible Study Teacher.

Shirley J. Ellis, TN: Husband Reverend Jim Ellis for over 30 yrs, they have 3 daughters. Trusted Jesus as Savior at age 13; involvement with Youth for Christ formalized decision to attend Detroit Bible Col; BA, Cornerstone U, degree in Social Studies and two minors, Bible and Religion; serves local church in various capacities; taught VBS, Sunday sch, and AWANA; teaches Women's Bible studies and wrote her own Bible study that she teaches to military officer wives; guest speaker for the MOPS program and Women's Retreat; Women's Ministry Dir.

Charlotte Ford, GA: Husband Joe Ford, Executive Dir of Int'l Prayer Ministries and pastor Oak Hill Bapt Ch, Lawrenceville, GA; children Brandon (Stephanie) Ford, Jennifer and Josh Turner and grandsons Eli Ford and Hampton Turner; graduated Valdosta State U; working on Masters at Southwestern Bapt Theo Sem; lives in Stone Mountain, GA.

Carol Gregory, PA: Husband Dr. Richard Gregory; 4 children; grandmother to 15; served as pastor's wife at Pennridge Community Ch, Perkasie, Pa; Braintrim Bapt Ch, Laceyville, Pa; and Limerick Chapel, Limerick, Pa; served as National Women's

Ministry Coordinator of IFCA Int'l, IFCA Int'l Conv Planner, Founder and Editor of Chera Fellowship Magazine for Widows.

Krissy Guhl, IL: Husband Scott Guhl, Senior Pastor of St. Olaf Lutheran Ch, Montgomery, IL; the couple is blessed with five sons.

Robin Hall, GA: Husband Dr. Ken Hall, Senior Pastor, First Bapt Ch of Lilburn, GA; the mother of two sons; she combines a job in real estate with a busy and fulfilling life of missions and teaching at the church.

Carol Henschel, GA: Husband Dr. Tommy Henschel, Senior Pastor in Ellerslie, GA; 4 children and 6 grandchildren; is Exec. Director of Sound Choices Pregnancy Clinic in Columbus, GA; has held similar positions throughout GA; Bible Study Ministry in the church; conducts women's conferences.

Melody Hertler, MI: Husband Pastor Chad Hertler at Central Bapt Ch, Flint, MI; mother of two sons. Graduated from Hannibal-LaGrange College with a Bachelor's Degree in Art.

Leah Hornok, IL: Grew up as a pastor's daughter in Salt Lake City, Utah; BA in Biblical Languages from Moody Bible Institute and is currently pursuing her MA in Biblical Exegesis from Wheaton College, where she works as a Resident Director. She hopes to continue in full-time ministry, using her Bible knowledge to teach others how to better follow God.

Janet Thompson Hoffman, LA: Husband Pastor Harvey Hoffman; 3 children and 4 grandchildren; pres, Nat'l Woman's Missionary Union (Southern Bapt Conv); is a teacher, speaker, and writer; lifelong member of WMU; resides near Farmerville, Louisiana with husband Harvey who is retired from full-time pasturing; the couple is now assisting the church family of nearby Enterprise Bapt Ch, where Harvey currently serves as interim pastor; BA, Baylor Univ; MA, New Orleans Bapt Theo Seminary.

Marcia Hornok, UT: Husband Pastor Ken Hornok, Midvalley Bible Ch, Salt Lake City; 6 grown children; graduate, Washington Bible Col; enjoys teaching God's Word through writing and speaking; her works have appeared in over fifty different publications; has written six curriculum books for young children; since

2001 she has been the managing editor of CHERA Fellowship, a quarterly magazine for people who have lost their mates (www.ifca.org and follow the links to Resources-IFCA Publications, CHERA Magazine, sharing CHERA with someone).

Patti M. Hummel, TN: Widow of Reverend Donald Reed Hummel, Sr.; 3 children; two granddaughters; educated at Moody Bible Institute, IL; UN, HI; author of 17 books; Int'l Speaker; Pres, The Benchmark Group LLC, Nashville, TN; member Community Bible Ch, Nashville, TN.

Dea Irby, GA: Husband Reverend Tom Irby, Senior Pastor, Christ Presbyterian Ch, Clarkesville, GA; 8 children and (so far) 6 grandchildren; a playwright and director/producer, teacher/speaker and a tea room café owner; she currently lives in the beautiful North Georgia Mountains with her husband and two youngest children as they serve Christ Presbyterian Church.

Lorie Looney Keene, KY: Husband Pastor Stephen Matthew Keene, Children's Minister, Pleasureville Baptist Church, Pleasureville, KY; Candidate for Doctor of Philosophy in Leadership, current student and M Div in Ed and Women's Ministries, the Southern Bapt Theo Seminary, Louisville, KY; BS in Nursing, Auburn U, Montgomery, AL; Assoc Dir of Women's Programs, the Southern Bapt Theo Seminary, Louisville, KY.

Jan Kimbro, NC: Husband Rev. Reggie Kimbro, pastor of Grace Free Presbyterian Church, Winston-Salem, NC: an adjunct professor of Biblical Interpretation at Geneva Reformed Seminary, Greenville, SC; 3 daughters; daughter of Dr. and Mrs. Richard Gregory, grew up in a pastor's home and graduated from Bob Jones U, Greenville, SC; women's conference speaker and writes for a women's periodical, A Quiet Heart.

Helen Krudop, MO: Husband Len Krudop, Pastor of Bethel United Methodist Ch, Wildwood, MO; involved in music ministry for years and currently serves as worship leader for Bethel's Praise and Gospel Service; certified through the American Assoc of Christian Counselors and assists her husband with counseling, prayer and shut-in ministries; teaches private piano lessons at West County Christian Academy, a Montessori School. Two grown children and 4 grandchildren.

Bonnie M. Lambert, GA: Husband Rev. Russell C. Lambert, SR Pastor, River Woods Baptist Ch, Bend, OR; 3 children; Children's Ministry Dir; Vacation Bible School Dir; Children's Ch teacher; Nominating Committee member; van driver for children; Webmaster and designer; Children's Sunday School and Bible Club teacher for over 30 yrs; personal secretary, bookkeeper and tax advisor; diploma from Institute of Children's Literature.

Jeannine Liebmann, MO: Husband Bob is Youth Pastor at St. Mark's Lutheran Ch in Eureka, MO; B.A. in Psychology, Concordia U, Mequon where Jeannine serves on the music team; M.A. in Professional Counseling from Lindenwood U; currently licensed in the state of Missouri and employed as a therapist in a hospital outpatient program.

Carolyn Lyon, PA: Husband Pastor Ross Lyon, First Bapt Ch of Allentown; 5 adult children, 13 grandchildren (#14 on the way); BA, Biblical Education, Columbia International U, Columbia, SC; worked two years with Child Evangelism Fellowship of Asheville, NC; retired after 25 years teaching in Lehigh Christian Academy, Allentown, PA; currently a Deaconess at First Bapt Ch of Allentown; also serving on Children's Ministry Team.

Lori Cherland McCune, ID: Graduated, Christian Heritage College (now San Diego Christian College). She and her husband are missionaries with American Missionary Fellowship, doing Latino church planting on the Idaho-Wyoming border.

Jewel A. McFarland, GA: Husband Rev. Robert E. (Bob) McFarland; pastor's wife for 19 yrs; 5 adult children; 4 of the children or their spouses are ministers on church staffs; 15 grandchildren; member of Oakwood Bapt Ch, Chickamauga, GA; Graduate of Theology, Tennessee Temple Schools; Bachelor of Religious Ed and Masters of Religious Ed, Covington Theo Seminary; served with husband for 22 yrs at Bethel Bible Village Christian Children's Home in TN; Volunteer: AAA Women's Service, Chattanooga, TN; Sonshine Ministry to shut-ins; at Covington Seminary, Fort Oglethorpe, GA 5 yrs as a Study Guide proofreader, Faculty Advisor, and English Prof.; Precept Bible study student for over 25 years.

Betsy Anne (Forbis) McSwain, NC: Husband Rev. Ronald W. McSwain pastor, Earlys Bapt Ch; retired School Teacher; AA, Wingate Col, NC; BA, Carson-Newman Col, TN; 1 year at Southern Bapt Theo Sem; working as Staff Assistany for Woman's Missionary Union of NC since '97 as Ministers' Spouses Support Coord; serving now: Board of NC Bapt Found; Chaplain of Ahoskie's Woman's Club and Chaplain of NC Retired Teachers' Assoc in our county.

Betty Mick, PA: Husband Reverend Kenneth Mick (www.lionslayer.com); 1 son, 4 daughters; has been a pastor's wife for 48 years. Besides serving together with her husband in five churches, Betty has taught elementary level in both Christian and public schools; B.A. in B.Ed. from Columbia International U, Columbia, SC.

Ellen Miller, Germany: Husband Reverend Terry Miller, church planting ministry in Germany (Bavaria); 4 children; born to Christian parents in Nashville, TN; accepted the Lord as Savior at age 12 at neighborhood VBS; BA in Christian Education, Bob Jones University.

Janet Miller, CO: Husband Roy, an ordained minister and counselor; 3 children; B.A. in Biblical Studies, CO, Christian U; Lay Ministry, Applewood Bible Church; Bible teacher to children, teens, and young adults for over 25 years; women's ministry: retreat speaker, Christian Women's Club speaker; 11 years as missionary with IMB (1993-2004), working with Internationals on the Cote d'Azur, France; helped to plant and ministered in churches in France.

Suzan Moyer, KS: Husband Reverend Greg Moyer; served the Federated Church of McDonald, KS for 29 yrs; degrees from Washington Bible Col and Fort Hays State U; while raising four sons taught voice and piano students; currently teaches 8th grade special ed in Kansas City.

Mary Englund Murphy, OK: Husband Pastor Bill Murphy, Calvary Bible Ch, Tulsa, OK; associates degree, Florida Bible Col; author of Winning the Battle of the Bulge: It's Not Just About the Weight; speaker for women's retreats, conferences, and special events.

Danelle Nelson, GA and Ukraine: Husband Reverend Steve Nelson (former pastor of Clemson Community Ch, SC); is presently serving as a missionary in Ukraine. She and her husband have 7 children and 2 grandchildren. Having homeschooled for 20 yrs in the Atlanta, GA area, she is now in the process of discovering God's new plans for her.

B. Michelle Patillo, VA: Wife of former Youth Pastor, mother of one son, member of East End Baptist Ch, currently pursuing Bachelors Degree in Religious Studies.

Kenyon Powers, SC and Ukraine: Husband Reverend Timmy Powers (former pastor of Clemson Community Ch, SC); serving with her husband as missionaries in Ukraine since 1998 with Great Commission Ministries, in evangelism, discipleship and church planting.

Georgia M. Sawhook, OH: Husband Pastor Tom Sawhook, Fellowship Bible Ch, Fairfield, OH; 7 children and 16 grandchildren; plays piano, soloist, and in the choir, directs Christmas programs, serves in VBS; women's conference Speaker; founder, manager of four Web Sites including a First Ladies in Ministry; author of Potty Training to Puberty—the Pitts!!! (with hugs along the way) at http://www.geocities.com/gsawhook/PottyPuberty.html.

Jacquelyn Sheppard, MO: Husband Reverend Glenn Sheppard; mother of 3 missionary children; still lives a busy life with 5 grandchildren and multiple "spiritual children" from her years of teaching and leading a high school; former newspaper and magazine writer, working on books; graduate of Mercer U in Macon, GA. Lives on a small farm with her husband where they raise a petting zoo for grandchildren; Bible and prayer conferences, national and internationally.

Dayna Street, TN: Husband Pastor Bill Street, Minister of Biblical Guidance at Bellevue Baptist Church in Memphis, TN, for 27 years; 2 sons, Jonathan and Matthew; Coordinator of Marketing and Enrollment for Continuing Studies at Union U.

Patti Toliver, MO: Husband Pastor Rich Toliver; raised in a Christian home, at the age of 5 trusted Christ as Savior; attended

Prairie Bible Institute, Three Hills, Alberta, Canada; graduated nursing sch as an LPN; they have ministered for twenty three years in Branson, MO; 4 children who are all married; home educated children through junior high: 4 grandsons; taught all age groups from small children to adult women. speaks at women's conferences and retreats.

Janice Upton, TN: Husband Pastor J.C. Upton; 3 adult children and 6 grandchildren; graduate Prairie Bible Institute, Christian ED and Missions & Biblical Studies; Covenant College, BA in Elementary ED; UT Chattanooga, Masters of ED/Special ED and Masters in Science; UT Knoxville, Masters Adult ED; currently enrolled UT Chattanooga seeking Endorsement in English as a Second Language; served with husband in Papua New Guinea;. served in ministry for evangelism, church planting, and discipleship in Namibia, South Africa with IBM.

Shirley Ann Unrau, Canada: Husband Pastor Pete Unrau; 4 adult married children, 10 grandchildren; BA, Briercrest Bible Col. She and Pastor Pete have served together for over 50 years, are on staff of Campus Crusade for Christ; they run Oasis Retreats. She speaks to ladies groups around the world and at Family Life Conferences across Canada. Author of Facing and Fighting Cancer, Help! I'm a Mother, How to Minister To Your Minister, The Role of Women.

Daisy Wong. CA: Husband Pastor Steve Wong, SR Pastor of Fellowship Bible Ch in Belmont, CA; 4 daughters. Raised in a Christian home, Daisy trusted Christ as her Savior in her young teens; soon dedicated her life to full-time ministry at a mission conference. Serving includes playing piano for worship, teaching Sunday School, discipling women; has started discipleship and "mommy walks" with her older girls and is immensely enjoying this new journey.

Robin Yawn, Nashville, TN: Husband Byron Yawn, Pastor at Community Bible Church, Nashville, TN; Bachelors Degree in Nursing from Mississippi Col. Robin and Pastor Yawn were high school sweethearts; they have three children Lauren, Wade, and Blake.

Notes

Notes